The Cattle Dog's Revenge

The Cattle Dog's Revenge

Bush Ballads and Yarns

Jack Drake

Central Queensland
UNIVERSITY
PRESS

First published in 2003 by Central Queensland University Press

Distributed by:
CQU Press
PO Box 1615, Rockhampton Queensland 4700
Ph: (07) 4923 2520
Fax; (07) 4923 2525
Email: cqupress@cqu.edu.au
www.outbackbooks.com

National Library of Australia

Cataloguing-in-Publication data:

Drake, Jack.

The cattle dog's revenge : bush ballads and yarns.

ISBN 978 1 876780 35 7.

1. Folklore - Australia.
2. Ballads, English - Australia.
3. Australian literature.
I. Title.

398.20994

Typset in 12 on 14.4 point Minion by Jane Dorrington
Printed by Watson Ferguson & Co. Moorooka, Brisbane.

Front cover photograph courtesy Sue Moore.
Back cover photograph copyright The Courier-Mail

Foreword

Jack Drake is everything that a good bush poet should be. Apparently Charles Dickens used to enthral audiences as he acted out his own wonderful novels. It was the same for me the first time I saw Jack perform his own poetry. I knew from the written word that the poems were great, but when I saw Jack, at Tenterfield 'Oracles of the Bush', perform *The Cattle Dog's Revenge*, I was just about ready to leap off my seat and give Woody a hand with the Rottweiler. I knew that here was a one-off, dead-set ripper act, young Jack Drake. Give him room!

Jack looks the part, and that helps. Henry Lawson and CJ Dennis would have written poems about Jack, for he has that spare bushman's frame, the laconic look that quickly sorts out the idiots, the easy speech, the uncompromisingly Australian colloquialisms. Which takes me to a point. There is a lot of friendly (sometimes not so friendly, at Bledisloe Cup time) rivalry between Australians and our cousins from The Shaky Isles. Jack Drake was born in New Zealand, yet I doubt that I've heard anything more 'Australian' than Jack's poetry. It's a bit like my wife Nerys Evans, and my good mate Eric Bogle. They have come from Wales and Scotland respectively, but they see things in Australia that I miss, because I take things for granted. Jack Drake is the quintessential bushman, because he lives the life at the same time as writing about it, and a New Zealand bushman comes from the same embryo as Clancy of the Overflow. In those halcyon days, the 1890s, Aussies and Kiwis shared a common ground in this remote southern region of the universe. The white people came mainly from England, Ireland, Scotland and Wales, and they inherited characteristics from the native Maori and Aboriginal people in much larger quantities than many of them realised. Out of it all came a unique melting pot of people who have no superiors in the world. There was so much common ground: you only have to read *The Bulletin* up to 1950 to see why Barry Crump and Henry Lawson had so much in common. There should be more literary exchanges to explore our similarities. The Rugby does the opposite, but that's OK.

Jack Drake has now elected to live permanently in Australia, and the number of prizes awarded to him and his poetry speak for themselves. May he keep performing, to all age groups. Oldies like me need to be revved up a bit, the young generation needs to be shown what fair dinkum Australia is all about. The freedom to perform will be possible for Jack Drake if the word gets around that this book is very worth buying.

I recommend *The Cattle Dog's Revenge* to all readers. The poems are magnificent, the themes are unique – here am I a Territorian and I sat amazed as I read *Diamond Eighty Eight* and wondered why I had not heard the story before. The language is colourful (!), evocative, and Jack's poetry ranges from hilarious (*Cattle Dog*) to the epic *(Diamond)* to the poignant (*Running Board Mick*). The prose stories give a vital diversity to the book. Once again, the language deserves to be read for its authenticity if for no other reason.

And I must say: "Goodonyermate" to old 'Silvertail', Professor David Myers, for producing and publishing this, and so many other worthwhile Australian books.

Ted Egan AM
ALICE SPRINGS

.

Acknowledgements

This book would not have happened without the help of my wife Stellamary Matheson Drake. Were it not for her hours of typing, correcting, support and criticism, you would now be rummaging through a carton of hand written rubbish.

Thanks also to Bruce Simpson and his brother Jeff who guided and encouraged my literary efforts. Had they not informed me of the existence of metre, my writing would be even more blatantly in feet and inches.

A big thank you to my friend Barney Belford for his proof reading abilities and some good ideas for poems.

Thank you to all my friends in The Australian Bush Poets Association who have been great sounding boards and sat through many hours of "Have a listen to this."

Last but certainly not least, my sincere appreciation to Ted Egan for his encouragement and for writing the Foreword, and to 'Old Silvertail' himself, David Myers, for having enough faith to publish.

— Jack Drake

Contents

The Cattledog's Revenge

If you've ever lived upon a farm, you'll know the feeling well.
How easy it can be to get the visitors from Hell.
Y'know those mongrels from the city that invite themselves to stay
Because they only want a holiday where they don't have to pay.

Now, I might be pretty cynical and I was just a kid,
But I'd seen it happen every year – it's what they always did,
Bring some ice cream and a box of fruit and half a slab of beer,
And act like it's a favour if they stay here half the year.

And all on the assumption that we'd be so glad to see
The half brother of our Uncle Harry's wife's third cousin Bea.
They never do a tap of work. They clean up all our grog.
But it all came to a screeching halt the year they brought the dog!

Yes, the middle seat was taken by this huge Rottweiler thing.
On his neck a studded collar without a hitching ring.
The old man stared in silence, then said '*You'll have to tie him up.*'
They said, '*He's had obedience training, and he's just the sweetest pup.*'

The dog bailed out the window. They said '*Oh you little tyke.*'
One word from this mug and he did exactly as he liked,
And like a black and tan tornado with a brainless, snarling face,
He caused an orgy of destruction 'round our peaceful country place.

He flogged our poor old kelpie bitch and not content with that,
Killed six of Mum's best laying chooks and murdered Grandma's cat.
He chewed our poor pet possum's tail and chased it up a tree
While this dork flicked pages in his book on 'Dog Psychology'.

And while the city bloke was trying to find answers out of books,
The Rottweiler, teeth gnashing, headed straight for Andy's chooks.
Yes, young Andy's special bantams who'd won prizes at the show,
Looked just like they were going to be the next thing here to go.

But Andy was a cunning lad with everything to gain.
He raced over to the kennels and let Woody off the chain.
And so to vindicate the honour of our simple country mutts,
Woody flew into the Rottweiler, and latched onto his nuts.

Now Woody is a cattle dog who's been around for years,
And for sportsmanship and honour, he won't get any cheers,
But he has one saving grace inside a multitude of sins.
By using every low trick in the book – Woody always wins!

From that useless flaming boofhead, there arose an awful howl.
They took off down the paddock at a thousand miles an hour
With Woody hanging grimly – his feet skidding in the dirt –
While my legs crossed all on their own, 'cause strewth, it must have hurt.

He swung hard between two saplings and set his own dog trap
When Woody sliding sideways, just failed to make the gap.
The bellows of the Rottweiler became a high pitched squeak.
He lost all interest in the flight, and sat down in the creek.

Then this poor mug from the city, he started acting tough
'till Dad roared in his face, *'You bum! I've had a bloody 'nough!*
Old Woody did the right thing. The proper thing to do!
Anyone who'd breed that mongrel, would be dumb as bloody you!'

And Dad's whole face went scarlet. His eyes flashed hard and mean.
He howled, *'I've seen some bludging mongrels, but you're the best I've seen!*
So pack your traps and snatch it, you rotten mongrel sod,
Or I'll make a wether out of you like Woody did your dog!'

With the air of people greatly wronged, they loaded their pet up
And bounced off down the driveway with that castrated pup.
But no more will we be troubled by those pushy city folk
Who inflict themselves upon you 'till it's gone beyond a joke.

And sometimes when the 'phone rings getting on towards Christmas time,
Dad's jaw begins to tighten as he's listening on the line.
Our grins keep getting wider. The Old Man begins to cough
Then roars, *'I've only got two words for you, and the second one is…..OFF!'*

Harvey's Toorak Tractor

Young Harvey was a Toorak lad, born upper crust you know.
That's just a term for half baked crumbs surrounded by loose dough.
But Harvey was alternative with a longing to be free
And no desire to work inside his father's company.

So Harvey left for Queensland with his girlfriend who was Jade.
Two kids born out of wedlock and another one half made.
They bought land through the Internet from an Agent way up there,
And Daddy paid the bill to keep them all out of his hair.

'Oh, my darling Jade', said Harvey. 'This is truly heaven sent.
We'll live with peace and love in a pristine environment.
We'll watch our children grow as one with flowers and with trees
As they frolic in the woodland with the birds and wallabies.'

'We'll live in perfect harmony. We'll bathe in crystal streams
And we'll be self sufficient. I'll grow lentils and mung beans.
I'll till the soil but I shun machinery of course.
So I'll be like the pioneers, and I'll plough with a horse.'

So Harvey bought a draft horse advertised in Country Life
From a horse dealer who told him it was driven by his wife.
It had ploughed and it had scuffled and pulled a forky slide,
And Harvey, trusting soul, believed horse dealers never lied.

Harvey caught his new toy, and prepared to break some ground.
He put the harness on the horse and drove it all around.
Went in and out between the trees and twice around the car.
Then backed him in and hooked the plough up to the swingle bar.

I suppose it would be cruel to call him just a Hippie Clown,
But Harvey put the gear on with the winkers upside down.
Dobbin snorted as he took the weight, and when he looked behind,
The mongrel bolted like a charger out of medieval times.

Jade meandered from the kitchen to smoke a joint outside.
She saw Harvey pass the homestead taking twenty metre strides.
'Oh Harvey, you look wonderful. Such style and such power!'
Then poor Harvey blew a sandal doing thirty ks an hour.

When the sandal twisted on his foot, that set the draft horse free.
Harvey shanghied off the reins and crashed into an Ironbark tree,
Then straight across the boundary fence at nearly fifty now,
Came a draft horse followed by a bouncing mouldboard plough.

Harvey tore his sandal off and wildly looked around,
Saw Dobbin in the distance fairly tearing up the ground.
Harvey muttered fiercely 'Where my draft horse goes, I goes'
Then leapt into the kombie van, blood streaming from his nose.

The van went through the broken fence at half the speed of sound,
With its blood-stained hippie driver, dander up and hammer down.
The plough was clearing suckers like a draft horse-powered stick rake.
Dauntless Harvey in the kombi van careering in its wake.

Straight towards a patch of scrub, the draft horse swinging wide.
Harvey ducked between the trees and pulled up alongside.
He dived upon the dragging reins, the cavalcade to slow,
Like a Champion Steer Wrestler at Mt.Isa Rodeo.

Harvey thoughtless of his safety, wrapped the reins around his hands
But his dreadlocks snagged the bumper of the flying kombi van.
Though it nearly bloody scalped him, he wouldn't cry enough
And snarling like a wolverine, young Harvey hung in tough.

The blood seeped from his naked scalp. Aw mate! It musta hurt.
He tried to dodge the bouncing plough sliding through the dirt.
Then the draft horse halted suddenly, and landed with a thump
When the plough flew over Harvey and hooked on a forky stump.

That mad horse struggled to its feet and backed out of the gear
With Harvey swinging off the reins, it threw the winkers clear.
Jade found Harvey dazed and bleeding as the day gave way to dark
And Dobbin joined a brumby mob out in the National Park.

Now Harvey's looking real sad — his hair is mighty thin.
A T-shirt full of busted ribs and missing lots of skin.
His poor old jaw is wired up. Jade feeds him with a spoon,
And Daddy looks like paying for a tractor fairly soon.

Horse Tailer

If you should travel westward where the inland rivers run
to where the wild budgies fly formations in the sun
towards the western sunset clothed in red, past 'Come by Chance'
where kestrels swoop and hover as the stately brolgas dance.

There you may see a travelling mob, the cattle feeding slow,
a sight that takes you backwards to the years of long ago.
The packhorse and the swag are now a truck and caravan.
But listen. Hear the horse bells tracking creeks that seldom ran.

Still, golden years of droving now consigned to ages gone,
have left their precious relics so the legends carry on.
Some only things that cannot speak, but some are living still,
and one lives down in my home town, his cottage by a hill.

Though limbs are frail and wasted now, his mind is sharp and clear.
It seems he's lived forever drifting on from year to year.
With time he'll paint a picture, measured speech drawled soft and slow
how beef came to our tables by the tracks old drovers know.

Tales told of wind and weather, bring the droving game to life,
slow days of gentle drifting, stormy nights of desperate strife.
That old voice rising, falling, weaves its spell in tales and quips,
breathing essence to our history in volleys of the whips.

Horse tailing was his specialty. His voice grows soft and kind.
Clear blue eyes twinkle merrily. Old favourites spring to mind.
He'll sketch a verbal picture of a clean limbed, brumby mare
or patient plodding packhorse humping camp ware way out there.

He speaks of mighty night horses. You almost seem to be
there riding on his dogwatch while the ringers eat their tea.
Low, droning song and padding hoof in evening's violet hush,
explodes in violent action when the wild store bullocks rush.

The team is leaping horseward as he chased the lead alone
that game horse flying nimbly through the brigalow and stone,
up shouldering the leaders in the scrub and broken ground.
'Son, I was just a passenger. That old horse turned 'em 'round.'

He's always glad to sit and yarn. We drink our mugs of tea
out underneath the branches of the pepperina tree.
I always stop to see him when I'm working fresh broke colts.
Last week he rigged my saddle with a greenhide monkey holt.

And shrewdly he evaluates each new moke's future worth.
Notes line of hip and shoulder and the depth of chest and girth.
I've learned so much of horses from this ageless droving man.
His slow drawl utters history from stock routes of this land.

He sits beneath his shade tree there, gnarled as a desert oak.
He'll talk if you will listen. He's a real 'fair dinkum' bloke.
I watch him scan the distance where the ridges meet the sky,
and know he's hearing horse bells by the soft look in his eye.

Lookin' After 'Orses

Forkin' up manure.
Pullin' tangled manes.
Seedy toe to cure,
Stood on fer yer pains.
Mixin' chaff and mashes.
Tightnin' clickin' shoes.
Dressin' cuts and rashes.
Man's got no flamin' clues.
Mud 'n rain one minute,
Next it's eat'n flies.
Dunno why I'm in it.
S'pose I'm tellin' lies.
Special kind of magic
Battling nature's forces.
'eart warmin' and tragic
lookin' after 'orses.

Feel yer spirit flyin'.
Watch 'em runnin' free.
Nothin' else worth tryin'.
Nowhere else to be.
Life's a flamin' puzzle.
Discontentment fades,
Touch of velvet muzzle
Between yer shoulder blades.
Silky lips a flutter
Up yer flamin' arm.
Makes yer melt like butter.
Can't resist their charm.
Cleaned a million stables,
Seen a thousand courses.
No designer labels
When yer lookin' after 'orses.

Degrees of Cooks

Inspect any station across this great Nation.
The cook will be somebody's wife.
Since the ladies took over, a stockman or drover
need no longer fear for his life.

But it wasn't that way in the battling old days
when cooks were a species apart.
They were rated by five if they kept you alive.
A *cook* was the one at the start.

Next came the *cookoo* who could make a fair stew
but damper replaced home made bread.
The roasts and the rest would be average at best
but at least everybody got fed.

Number three was a slayer they called a *baitlayer* —
an unclean and scurrilous lout.
His curries and stews were a glutinous ooze.
His roasts had the blood seeping out.

If Baitlayers were bad, *tucker muckers* were mad.
Their dampers were lumps of raw dough.
And the word I've called 'mucker' also rhymes with 'Tucker.'
I can't say it — the children you know.

But on top of the heap, that detestable creep,
that evil unsavoury cur
shouldn't cook for a dog. Soaked in vice, dirt and grog
they knew as *wilful murderer.*

He smelled like a skunk, was perpetually drunk.
Men lived on raw meat and burnt flour.
They would run at each end and their workday expend
squatting out on the flat by the hour.

For the worker today, a fine breakfast is laid.
At smoko there's biscuits and scones.
And the lunches and teas send old hands to their knees
to thank God the good old days are gone.

The Whistlestop Hotel

I met her in the carpark at the Whistlestop Hotel.
She climbed out of a dusty red sports car,
Blue jeans wrapped 'round long, long legs. God they fitted well.
Face and figure like a movie star.
I said *'Baby are you going in? I'd love to buy you one,*
maybe dance a bit and shoot some pool,
'cause I've been up the country ringing cattle in the sun
and right now I'm red hot to play the fool.'

We drank and danced the night away. I held her as she swayed.
She whispered in my ear *'You dance so well.'*
As the jukebox played those country songs, she stole my heart away
and I loved her at the Whistlestop Hotel.

In the glory of an outback dawn down by the riverside,
we wandered through the cypress hand in hand.
Face pressed in her long tresses I whispered *'Be my bride?'*
but she smiled and said *'Boy, you don't understand.*
I come from the big city, daughter of a wealthy man,
and I just took off for a day or two.
Next week I'm s'posed to marry. That's the reason why I ran.
My life could never suit a man like you.'

'So hold me tight my darling, while the morning star still shines,
then leave me to the life I know so well.'
She gave me her young body on the ground beneath the pines
and I lost her near the Whistlestop Hotel.

We parted in the morning sun. I watched her drive away,
her dust the wake of passing ships at night,
heart hanging heavy in my chest to greet the newborn day.
How wrong could something be that felt so right,
and Lord I hope she's happy with her money and her place
rubbing shoulders with the wealthy at the club.
But if she ever travels through this land of endless space,
does she think about the ringer from the scrub?

Since then I've lived and loved out in the sunlit lands afar.
I woo'ed and won a lovely western belle,
but sometimes in the grey dawn when I see that morning star,
I dream about the Whistlestop Hotel.

Clear Brown Eyes

When the shadows crowd the corners 'neath the harsh electric light,
From the doorways and the alleys creep the creatures of the night
Where a country girl will take her place once more to live the lies
And gaze, weary at the world, through a pair of clear brown eyes.

All the bridges she left burning as line after line she crossed
In her odyssey of pain to join the legions of the lost,
Embracing thrill and wild rush, forsaking counsel wise
While the haunted rings of shadow grow beneath those clear brown eyes.

The reckless roads she travelled since she left the family farm
Are written like a road map in the tracks upon her arm.
Though she's nothing but a plaything men use and then despise,
Still a hint of something finer hides within those clear brown eyes.

For what can it be that drove her to the needle and the street
In flashy clothes and makeup as she pounds her nightly beat?
But all the sin and degradation still cannot quite disguise
A legacy of country locked into those clear brown eyes.

And I wonder could she ever come to sing and laugh again
Before the drugs and clients wreck her body and her brain.
And will she miss those endless lands out where the eagle flies
Before the last light turns to darkness behind those clear brown eyes.

The Cattle Dog's Return

I suppose you've heard my story when the bludgers came to stay
and how Dad and Woody sent the city dwellers on their way.
How an old and mangy, blue dog made their pampered pet a dud
and ruined all his chances of advancement as a stud.

Dad still laughs and smirks about just how the job was done.
Woody scratches fleas contentedly while dozing in the sun.
And we've branched into horticulture. We're developing new breeds.
There's a young Rottweiler Nut tree down where Woody spat the seeds.

The fruit is small and egg shaped and the flesh is rather dark.
The tree trunk's thick and solid and carries lots of bark.
We built a fence around it and we tied it up on stakes
but whenever Woody pees on it, it quivers and it shakes.

We were seeking out new markets, expectations running high
and a Government Agronomist sent by the DPI
was skilled in nut production and would tell us what to do
but his arrival was accompanied by a sense of Deja Vu.

A four by four bounced up our drive and stopped outside the door
and everybody got the feeling that we'd all been there before.
A city bloke behind the wheel in clothes so clean and neat
and a bloody great Rottweiler dog beside him on the seat.

With jutting jaw the old man muttered '*Here we go again.*'
Woody howled and snarled and growled and nearly broke his chain.
The chooks were heading for the trees. Our tail-less possum cowered
as Dad ground out his ultimatum '*City dogs are not allowed!*'

'*Oh come now, my dear fellow. I've bred these dogs for years.*
She's gentle as a kitten. You need not have any fears.
And this one is my finest flower — the pick of all my breed'
but the old man was quite adamant. '*You keep her on a lead!*'

Then Woody stopped his snarling and his nose began to twitch.
I reckon he'd just worked out that the Rottie was a bitch.
Now with both the canine genders Woody's had a lot of luck.
It's all the same to Woody, be it fight or be it ... frolic.

Then Mum said *'Tie the dog up and before you see the tree*
come on in the kitchen and we'll have a cup of tea.'
He said, *'I'll just tie my darling up and give her water first*
then I'd love a country smoko for we've both worked up a thirst.'

Dad let out the smirk that he'd been trying not to show
and whispered *'Andy just duck over there and let old Woody go.*
We don't need Rottweilers 'round here. Let's nip this in the bud.
We'll improve his breeding program with a dash of blue dog blood.'

We had a cuppa then the expert said *'We must be getting on'*
and smilingly he strolled outside full up with tea and scones.
But his demeanour changed dramatically as he walked outside the gate
for there was Woody and the Rottie in a compromising state.

It was plain to see his pet show dog was firmly in disgrace
and Woody had a mongrel grin plastered on his face.
'You shameless little hussy. You're heading for the vet.
I'll send someone else to check your tree for I'm just too upset!'

'Her offspring's all pre-sold' he wailed. *'You've fouled my program up.'*
Dad said *'Woody's pretty handy so they should be decent pups.*
He guards the ute. He's good on stock and death on feral hogs.'
While young Andy filled a bucket up to separate the dogs.

So as one more messed up city dog went bouncing down the track.
The whole family burst out laughing 'cause it brought old memories back.
And when asked if Woody always wins, I'd have to say *'My oath!*
There's been two Rottweilers on our place and Woody's stuffed 'em both!'

Diamond Eighty Eight

Jim Campbell was a boy from out of early New South Wales
Riding hard like some before him. A Trooper on his trail.
He'd left the home farm bareback on a young unbroken horse
Just ahead of some attention by the local police force.

To call the lad Jim Campbell here is slightly premature.
When Jim fled New England, he was known as Sonny Muir.
To fellows on the outside track, a name has little clout.
They tend to judge you by your worth when you get further out.

In Ninety-three to Katherine, Jim Campbell he came through
With a mob of good blood horses branded Circle W.
It made the northern locals laugh and whistle through their teeth.
The brand was Peter Warburton's – Commissioner of Police.

You could only but admire the man for his infernal cheek.
He sold them to the Chinese scratching gold around Pine Creek.
Chinese miners think of gold and little else besides
And have not the slightest interest in marks on horses' hides.

Now Jim, he put some time in camping in the river bend
And every man in Katherine Pub was glad to call him friend.
He had his spree and left them with a thousand miles to ride,
His eye on squatters' horses in the country back inside.

Almost three years to the day, he walked back in the bar
And 'round a pot of Katherine beer, he draped his handlebar.
He blew the froth from his moustache, said '*Boys, I'm here to stay,
For things are far too hot for me a thousand miles away.*'

He did some years of freighting for the O'land Telegraph,
But plodding by the bullocks didn't tend to make him laugh.
So once again, the larrikin in Campbell's soul arose.
He took to poddy dodging with his dusky lady, Rose.

Rose and he moonlighted cleanskin cattle by the score.
She saved his bacon more than once in brushes with the Law.
She gave O.T. his son, to him in the ranges wild,
But died by Katherine River bearing Campbell's second child.

Throughout the next wet season, very little work was done.
Jim spent it planning to fulfil ambitions for his son.
He used the *Illawarra* block beyond the Murranji,
Its owner living far away in Collarenabri.

Now Jim was a runholder. Little O.T. was his mate.
He registered his station brand — the Diamond Eighty Eight.
It had a stroke of genius a larrikin would love.
'Vic.Rivers' famous G.I.O. — It fitted like a glove.

Soon he took some partners in to do the station jobs
And scoured the big runs' boundaries picking up the cleanskin mobs.
But partnerships breed discontent and Jim got itchy feet.
He sold out of *Illawarra* and moved to *The Retreat*.

And there by Battle Creek on that remote and wild block
A supernatural increase occurred with Campbell's stock.
But all the Northern Terrors grinned and didn't find it odd.
They knew Jim would burn the Eighty Eight on the Lamb of God.

He reaped his harvest off the absentee owned companies.
The one he hit the hardest was the big run – 'V.R.D.'
Now the older hands will tell you *Victoria River Downs*
Had their brand changed to the Bull's Head while Campbell was around.

But Jim fell in bad company. It made the old hands sad
To see a horseman, a bushman and a good man go to bad.
From a duffing virtuoso with his instrument — the brand,
Jim became a cattle thief. He used the frying pan.*

The frying pan's a blotch job. Not a thing a man should do.
His mates rode down from Katherine and told him that much too.
They cursed him for his greed but now the damage had been done.
The Troopers had the word, and once more Jim was on the run.

They raided *The Retreat* but Jim had bushed the mob and gone
To the one place where they wouldn't look — Old Port Essendon,
While a little deaf mute maiden with the unkind name 'Dummy',
Led Troopers on a goose chase where Victoria meets the sea.

Throughout the cattle country, Campbell tales were running thick.
A cross between Ned Kelly and some Yankee Deadwood Dick
Was the sort of desperado they made Jim out to be.
Prepared to shoot at any Trooper who should risk his liberty.

At signs of Life or shipping Jim would simply fade away
'till the day Alf Brown's old lugger came thrashing up the bay.
Alf knew nothing of the uproar that caused Campbell to hide.
He'd just spent two years trading on the Northern Queensland side.

Jim Campbell stepped from hiding and to Alf the tale was told
And Trader Brown was not surprised, for he knew Jim of old.
Alf reckoned that the Port was not the safest place to be
And moved them to Malay Bay on the Arafura Sea.

They camped under some tamarinds where mangrove swamps were thick,
Jim and O.T., the faithful Nellie and her husband Dick.
The elders of the Yerrakool met them beneath the trees.
They forged a bond of friendship with the Aborigines.

There in that tropic paradise the family settled down,
Their hauls of pearl and trepang sold for them by Trader Brown.
And Jim the poddy dodger, learned to love the ocean sand
As he faded from the white man's world in wild Arnhem Land.

But Paradise is temporary and trouble rose again
In a stripling known as Nundil — white reared and mission trained.
He infiltrated Jim's mob and the Myall band as well,
And gradually convinced them Campbell was a fiend from Hell.

With sly manipulation, he convinced the Myall band
That all of their misfortunes were caused by Campbell's hand.
With subtle inference, he played the tribesmen for a fool
To unleash the tribal murderers within the Yerrakool.

One night Jim gathered trepang like a hundred nights before
As the grey mud-daubed assassins came slinking down the shore.
Painted torsos gleaming as the torchlight pierced the dark.
He faced them as a spearhead took him underneath the heart.

The 'Diamond's' breath was failing fast. His eyes began to close
As from his bleeding breastbone, he tore the shovel nose.
Four more spears came thudding, rending flesh and letting blood,
And Jim, he fell a dead man, face down in the mangrove mud.

His faithful friends, they packed the camp and travelled overland
Using horses Jim had caught and broke from wild brumby bands.
They met up with Bill Murphy — Warden of the Northern Coast,
And he gave Jim a burial much lonelier than most.

Near the mouth of the King River lies a lowly ring of stones
That Murphy piled on Jim to keep the dingoes from his bones.
Not far from where 'The Diamond' turned to make his final stand
Now lies that lost and lonely grave up there in Arnhem Land.

Someday by the Arafura Sea some wanderer may find
Some cattle-country history that the world has left behind.
They may chance upon the implement that sealed Jim Campbell's fate.
A rusted branding iron that reads the Diamond Eighty Eight.

*   The 'frying pan' is a blotch applied over the top of an existing brand, suitable to fool a Jackaroo on a galloping horse.

'Buck-Off' Bungie

A lot of people reckoned Bungie was a bit slow, but they hadn't bothered to look past first impressions. There was nothing slow about Bungie except the way he walked and talked and his general athletic co-ordination.

Bungie was a mild mannered, gentle bloke who looked at bit like Radar O'Reilly, and was physically the toughest man I ever saw. The first time we saw him, he turned up at a rodeo on a little hundred CC motorbike and entered all the second division rough stock events.

He was a thick set, short legged, roly poly sort of a bloke who didn't have one bit of natural ability. He was clumsy and uncoordinated but he had more 'try' than ten men, and in the rodeo arena, an ounce of 'try' is worth a ton of ability any day.

He got on his bareback horse and it ironed him out right outside the gate. To be fair on him, the nag was far too good for a novice contest, but as time unfolded we found out the old Bungie had a knack of drawing the rankest stock in the pen with uncanny regularity.

The saddle bronc he tried lifted him higher than the bareback one had, and Bungie hit the dirt with a thump that made the whole crowd sort of collectively wince. His bull riding effort is probably better not mentioned and when his little bike puttered out of the grounds, the boys at the bar all reckoned that was the last we'd see of that bloke.

Next week the sort of cross country family, that makes up the ranks of the rodeo riding community, pulled up in another town and there was Bungie and his little bike. Three more head of stock. Three more good draws and three more buckoffs.

It went on like that all season. Bungie getting on. Bungie nodding for the gate. Bungie getting off. Pretty soon everyone from green rookies to the best of the open competitors would flock to the rails as soon as his name was called. He was the gamest, most resilient coot any of us had ever laid eyes on. He even developed his own unofficial fan club, and the announcers started calling him 'Buck-off Bungie'.

The crowd would wait on his short performances with bated breath. A sort of group groan would ripple around the arena as the best horse or bull in the draw launched him skywards and only tailed off when he crashed into the dirt with a thump that seemed to shake the whole place.

Top line bull and bronc riders had been known to wander off after another one of his chuteless skydives shaking their heads and muttering, '*I'd win the world if I could only draw stock like that son of a bitch can.*'

Most of the blokes who were winning ran rodeo schools wherever they could, and Bungie always paid his money and lined up ready and willing to get bucked off as many times as stock and daylight would allow.

Schools usually sorted out the men from the boys in the novice ranks, and most blokes would get on three or four head then lose interest. Not our Bungie. He'd heave himself out of the dirt for another try as long as they'd run stock up for him, and most times the instructor would quit before he would.

A time event hand called Larry Looper who was always keener on making money than friends, talked him into having a go at bulldogging so he could get a cut at Bungie's bank account. He carted him off to his place one Sunday and Bungie leaped off a running bulldogging horse at thirty two steers that afternoon in Looper's practice arena and never caught one of them. Even Bungie was reeling a bit after that little effort and so was his bank book after Larry charged him five dollars a head.

We all got to know him that season, and he made a lot of friends through his pleasant, self-effacing manner and the raw guts and tenacity of the man. Bungie never said much about his home life and I suspect he might have had an unhappy childhood. It stands to reason that anyone who could soak up punishment the way he could, had probably spent a fair bit of time being abused.

Everyone worth knowing on the circuit did their best to help him and it became a bit of a crusade among us all to see Bungie get one rode. He was getting tuition from nearly all the top competitors and at the last show before the finals, he drew a head of stock he had a chance with.

'Ace-hi' was a money bull. He went well up and looked good, but he wasn't too strong and had no nasty twists or cut-backs to worry about. I don't reckon Bungie ever considered winning, but he'd been dreaming about just being on top when the buzzer sounded, as long as we'd known him.

The National Bullriding Champion tied Bungie's hand down and although the crowd wouldn't have known it, there was an electric air 'round the chutes and every cowboy there was riding that bull right along with the old Bungie.

The gate swung and 'Ace-hi' bailed out steep like he always did. Bungie leaned into his riding hand and as the bull levelled out at the top of his leap, a ragged cheer went up from the boys as he threw his free hand back behind his head and grabbed with both his spurs. He got a bit off his hand* on the next buck, but something had finally clicked in our mate's head, and his balance hand whipped across in front of him as Bungie got properly tapped off* and 'Ace-hi' never had a chance after that.

The hooter sounded like an Angels' Chorus to us, so God only knows how good it sounded to the boy on the bull. Getting off had never been a problem for Bungie and he left with a grin from ear to ear as a motley crew of jeans and dusty cowboy hats charged down the arena in a yelling, hand shaking, back slapping mob.

We took him from the arena on our shoulders. The applause was deafening and we didn't put him down 'till the cavalcade reached the bar. A slightly shell shocked Bungie found himself with a beer in one hand and a double rum in the other. He'd worked harder and fallen harder than most champions ever do to get that bull ridden and that night nothing could wipe the delighted grin off Bungie's face. Aw yeah, he won too.

He found a home in rodeo and the cowboys and cowgirls, who can be a standoffish bunch with people who don't fit their code, opened their ranks to him.

Next year he came back stronger than ever. He still got more than his share of buckoffs, but he got a few rode as well and sometimes he even took home a little money. I'll never forget Bungie. There was no way he was ever going to win a title and he certainly wasn't cast in the mould of the classic cowboy hero, but for try and tenacity, I've never seen his equal. If they gave out titles for guts alone, Bungie would have won the world.

---

* 'off his hand' is when a rider in a bull or bareback ride is sliding back instead of sitting up close to the hand holding on.

* 'tapped off' is when a rider finds his seat in a rough stock contest early in the ride.

To Own a Horse

Through uncounted centuries, your hard hooves cut the earth.
In dim, Jurassic forests, a young world gave you birth.
Victim of the predator in countless violent scenes,
Metamorphosed through the ages to produce the equine genes.

Through stages of development, you stepped into the light
Gentle herbivore emerging from the forests of the night.
Pearl of evolution, grace and power creating force
Designed for speed and motion.   You became the noble horse.

What primeval situation caused the circumstances when
You blended your lifestyle with the selfish dreams of men?
Is there some deep seated instinct that has lurked within your breed
That made you bow to slavery, to lend your grace and speed?

What can be the connection that has linked your life with Man
When in freedom and unfettered on the open Steppes you ran?
What made you bow that gentle head? By what means were you woo'ed
To accept the bit and bridle, and the yoke of servitude?

Did love reward your sacrifice to keep the exchange square?
Would horses truly state that man has held the bargain fair?
If man would keep a friend like you, please understand he must
Keep faith with Gods of Equus. Never break that sacred trust.

The horse is tied to mankind. You rely on us for life,
And sadly in our careless world, neglect of you is rife.
You have no means to protest cruelty, ignorance or greed.
With all the gifts you bear us, are we there to fill your need?

If we allow your well being and maintenance to slip
We are just as cruel and brutal as a fiend who plies a whip.
Embrace your care. Accept your costs. Reject violence and force.
If we bear this duty willingly, we're fit to own a horse.

'P' Day Invasion

I'm just a little possum and at night I like to roam
in a patch of Aussie bushland with a gum tree for me home.
But I've just been rudely 'woken after snoozin' peacefully.
Some mongrel with a chainsaw was cuttin' down me tree!

Some dopey flamin' woodhawk messin' up a good day's sleep!
Just bowl a man's apartment to replenish his wood heap!
They catch yer while yer sleepin' I always seem to find.
I just wish the stupid buggers were nocturnally inclined.

I dashed out on a handy branch and tried to pee on him
(me last act of defiance as the homestead altered trim),
then that clawing, clutching death ride, the bit I hate the most,
worse than any roller coaster at a theme park on the Coast.

The breaking branches launch yer. When yer land, yer cop a thump.
How'd you like it with no leg rope on a slingshot bungy jump?
Tenth time I've been evicted. It's beyond a blasted joke,
and I'm getting fairly cranky for a peaceful little bloke.

So beware the Possum Rising when the crack, fur clad brigade
starts to slink out of the forest to silently invade.
When plastic parts on chainsaws will be gnawed by angry teeth,
and the tins of fuel and chain lube are punctured underneath.

The tyres on the utes will all be savagely attacked
like the goggles and the ear muffs, you can take that for a fact,
and anything that we can wreck. We've had it up to here!
The time of the Uprising's getting very, very near.

Then the vengeance of the possum will be shouted from the trees
as the chainsaws are all struck down by marsupial disease.
Tree borne, night trained terrorists who sneak and sabotage
nothing safe or sacred in each tool shed or garage.

So beware you weekend wood hogs as you sharpen up your saws,
there's a rustling in the gumtrees and a clash of teeth and claws.
Nocturnal squads are drilling to make home destroyers pay
when piles of broken chainsaws mark the dawning of.....P DAY!

The Possum

Rustler was a raking grey and handy on a beast
But he wasn't any kid's horse. He was tight to say the least.
If the slightest thing upset him, he'd drop his head and buck.
The old grey horse was tough enough. A rider needed luck.

To keep a leg on each side with Rustler at his peak
(he wasn't short on practice for he'd blow ten times a week)
Was a trick that took some beating. Right now I seemed to be
A little on the down side. Six to him and four to me.

I strolled 'round the holding paddock on Rustler's back one day
To find a broken fence wire where a bull had got away.
The dogs put up a possum in a patch of bracken fern.
The brush tail climbed the grey's front leg and man, he threw a turn!

We left the ground a shaking, Rustler's head between his knees.
He was going to lose the possum and that included me.
Thin skinned as Rustler was, those claws were giving him some pain.
We whipped and snapped and clattered like a broken windmill chain.

The way the horse was bucking told me soon I would be gone.
I felt that dread condition called 'the Round Arse' coming on.
Every rider knows the feeling when the horse is too damn rough.
He skyed me fair and simple with the possum hanging tough.

I hit the dirt a-rolling just the way that I'd been trained
A Stringy-bark got in the way and caused a stabbing pain.
I watched the horse high rolling marsupial on his side,
And gave credit to the possum 'cause that furry cove could ride.

The possum stuck like plaster 'till the grey horse finally stopped
At the bottom of the paddock in the distant view I copped.
Then that possum dismounted (as I hobbled painfully),
Glanced scornfully at Rustler and climbed a nearby tree.

Though he had the great advantage of four spurs every boot,
You can't take it off that possum. He could really sit a root!
Although he never rode before, he hung up through that strife.
Perhaps his name was Skuthorpe in a long forgotten life.

In the years I've spent with horses, I've rode every kind of prad,
Showed off upon the soft ones, hung and rattled on the bad,
But I've never slung a leg across a four hoofed power keg
Like the whirlwind that was Rustler with the possum up his leg.

Shearing in the Nudist Club

Now, I'm really quite a shy bloke and I'd never entertain
The thought of running naked through the woodland and the plain,
But there's people who think clothes are just not needed in the scrub.
That's how I got this job of shearing in a nudist club.

This ad. was in the paper for someone who could keep
A handpiece in the wool and peel about a hundred sheep.
She'd be just the thing for Saturday, so it seemed to me.
I could cop a hundred dollars and be in the Pub by three.

I sat there by their gateway in the old ute's driver's seat
And read the sign that claimed this was a 'Naturists' Retreat'.
'*This must be a mob of greenies. I'll have some fun,*' I thought
'Cause winding up Tree Huggers is a common rural sport.

I poked down to the woolshed sitting out there on the flat.
Unpacked me gear and wondered idly where the boss was at.
'*Hi there*' said a voice behind me. I started at the sound.
I nearly dropped me bundle when I flamin' turned around!

This bloke stood there before me with a grin upon his dial
And not one stitch of clothing on, of any shape or style.
'*I am so pleased to see you. You must be our shearer man.
I'll call up all the others, and we'll help you all we can.*'

Some were fat and some were wrinkly, and some could use a feed.
My face glowed like a tomato as I set the cutter's lead.
I slid the handpiece on the tube and locked it with a twist
As silently I wondered '*Could I take much more of this?*'

I dragged the first ewe from the pen and peeled the belly wool.
The nudies stared and Ooohd and Aahd. I felt just like a fool.
I kept my head down so that I would not be forced to see
Those boobs and bums and naughty bits in close proximity.

They were saggy. They were baggy, but one or two were prime.
The little naked tar boy, he was working overtime.
For I mostly kept my eyes shut my sanity to keep.
Be they beautiful or ugly, I still cut the flamin' sheep.

My throat was dry. My breath was short. My sweat was running free
And I nearly got my jaw broke by a swinging mammary.
A bum cheek poked into my ear. My fear became intense
And I prayed its big fat owner wasn't plagued by flatulence.

The women who picked up the wool, they were a wicked pair.
One had the look of paradise, the other dark despair.
The young rousy was an art form constructed to bewitch,
But the old one was a ringer for an ancient Bull Dog bitch.

They picked up fleeces each in turn — the beauty and the crone.
I swear when that old girl bent over, I shore by feel alone.
But when the young one picked the fleece, I shore from memory
For I had wonders to behold that shearers seldom see.

Every second sheep I shore, I showed my style in full
But my head was in the brisket when the old girl took the wool.
Still, I came to see the nudists in a rather different light.
With sheilas like her 'round the place, I'd pay me fees tonight.

I shore their sheep and waited. Didn't go down to the Pub.
She took me by the hand and showed me 'round the Nudist Club.
When she hugged me tight and kissed me and gazed into my eyes,
Any doubts I had, they vaporised and drifted to the skies.

I stayed and celebrated with the nudies all that night.
I'd promised all my life to her before the morning light.
The trouble was, I found out with the rising of the sun,
The old girl was her *mother!* Oh my God ! What had I done?

Realities of War

Dad was not a combat soldier, but he played his part as well.
Hauling ammo to the front, he saw his share of shot and shell.
The only things he'd talk about were the mateship and the fun
but not a word about the bloodshed and the harvest of the gun.

I listened to the stories he and his old mates would say
when I drove him to the Service and the Pub on Anzac Day.
They'd laugh about the navvie tricks and rat bag digger pranks
but to their fallen comrades they just willed their silent thanks.

Still with the gory fascination of an inexperienced kid
I passed them beers and tried to glean the secrets that they hid.
My Wild West mentality craved to hear the things they saw,
but by mute consent, they covered the realities of war.

Then my Dad's mate Trevor Parker, led me quietly away
and said *'Jack, the things you want to know are better left to lay.*
We understand the questions of the ones who were not there
but forcing memories on the ones who were, simply isn't fair.'

'That's why none of us like talking of the horrors that we saw.
All that 'Death or Glory' bullshit has no real place in war.
I hope you never load and fire as shells tear up the ground
splattered with your best mate's blood, while death is all around.'

'May God decree you never see your friend sprawled in the clay
shot to bits and crying for a mother far away.
Chopped down by machine gun fire and pleading to be dead
as rifles crackle viciously and shells whine overhead.'

Then Trevor Parker stammered and forced himself to say
how he held his mate's intestines in while life force ebbed away,
and I felt acute embarrassment and shame washed over me
when tears poured down his face 'cause I'd unleashed the memory.

'Mr. Parker, Christ I'm sorry' I mumbled in my shame.
He clasped me by the shoulder and said *'Son, war's not a game.*
I understand your interest, that's why I took you to one side,
but it hurts too much to talk about the ones of us who died.'

He said *'If you hear a soldier skite and glorify the War*
you can bet he worked behind a desk in admin. or the store.
The ones who fought up at the front, won't have too much to say'
and we both dragged out our hankies and wiped our tears away.

We walked back in the bar and Dad glanced at us as we came.
He was laughing at a yarn about a Crown and Anchor game
and the look that passed between them there, Trevor and my Dad,
confirmed he knew about the little talk that we just had.

Since then I've had occasion to observe some Army types
Peace time soldiers declaiming their gung ho service hype.
They're but a shallow imitation of the men who went before.
Those facing live rounds knew the true realities of war.

And they wouldn't talk about it, all the carnage and the pain.
They just picked up the pieces and got on with life again.
So I'm sorry you old diggers, for my tactless crass mistake.
I see now that you're all heroes like my Father, Alec Drake.

Now each Anzac Day I cheer them and for me there is no doubt
when I see the old men marching some with medals, some without.
I respect how they all suffered and the gift to us they gave
but the realities of War those men will carry to the grave.

The Green Knob

The tale of the green knob is a story you should know.
It happened to yours truly not so very long ago.
I headed out towards the west to buy myself a ute.
They don't get too much rust out there. I'll get a real beaut.

I pulled into a car yard in a little western town.
Saw a sweet Kingswood one-tonner and laid my money down
After arguing a lot about the merits of the car
With a dealer who was smarmy as car dealers most are.

Now I had a ute that I could say was fit to drive around.
I do this every few years when I drive one in the ground.
But one thing caught my attention — a green knob on the dash
With a slide and two positions. One for slow and one for fast.

I drove back towards the mountains rapt in my new transport mode.
It cruised along so easy, fairly seemed to love the road.
But the green knob had me going. I just had to play with it.
When I put it down from slow to fast, I nearly had a fit!

The ute took off like crazy. Went from fifty to the ton.
It immediately doubled the speed that it had done.
I shot the damn thing back again. It started to shut down.
Quite a handy little gadget but I'll use it out of town.

So I fooled around at low speeds and I'll tell you it's a rush
From forty up to eighty with a god 'almighty thrust.
But I doubt I'll use it often. That I'm fairly free to say.
It tore bloody miles off the tyres each time it leapt away.

But after my old tractor, this sleek new beast felt grand.
I came upon one of those straights out on the level land.
I was getting fairly cocky, so I pushed it up a bit
Then I glanced into the mirror. My heart dropped and I said '*Shit!*'

'Cause from out behind a billboard came a copper on a bike
And he must have wanted me, for there was no one else in sight.
I saw him jump the spoon drain. His light was flashing blue.
I thought '*I've got just the weapon to confuse hell out of you.*'

A thousand c.c. monster carrying a Hitler clone
Came screaming up behind me, after me and me alone.
So I thought '*It's now or never.*' I jerked the green knob down
And I felt a few G-forces as the Kingswood left the ground.

We went tearing down the Highway twice a hundred thirty k's
Which makes two sixty to the hour if I'm not in a daze.
The bike and copper dropped away like they were standing still
Then the white lines racing at me, my vision seemed to fill.

Then my conscience started niggling. '*If he got your plate, you're gone.*
To try and bolt, a man would have to be soft in the scone.
If you've any brains, go back and face the fickle gods of fate.'
They've nothing else upon me. I've been pretty good of late.

About two k's back along the road the bike was plain to see.
It had speared straight through a Cocky's fence and landed in a tree.
The cop was by the Highway with no sign that he'd been hurt
Sitting there upon his helmet and doodling in the dirt.

By some fluke we'll never know, he barely had a scar.
A cut upon his left hand and some grazes from the tar.
His uniform was knocked around. He had a dusty air
But his face bore the appearance of someone who wasn't there.

His diction slow and halting, he looked up and spoke these words
Mad eyes staring wildly with a countenance absurd.
'*I was hard upon his hammer almost reaching for my book*
When the stinkin' rotten bike stopped. So I got off for a look!'

'Mulga Bill' — The Sequel

Great Grandad lived at Eaglehawk just two miles down the road
From where the famous 'Mulga Bill' that wild bike bestrode.
And my Dad said that his Grandad would very often speak
How 'Mulga' never left that outlaw bike in Deadman's Creek.

'Mulga Bill', he was a horseman, a rider of great fame,
And one bolt down a mountain wouldn't make him quit the game.
Horseman's Honour is a trait that comes from fortitude within,
So 'Mulga' wheeled the cycle home to try and break it in.

He tied it to a stock yard with a piece of greenhide rope.
To save from getting kicked or struck, put hobbles on the spokes.
Then all around and over, he bagged it with a sack
And gingerly he eased himself across its narrow back.

His buttocks clenched the saddle and his feet the pedals found.
He slipped the rope and waited 'till the outlaw left the ground.
As Banjo told us, there was nothing 'Mulga' couldn't ride,
So it seemed an anti-climax when the bike fell on its side.

He walked around the prostrate bike and watched it lying there.
'Mulga' cursed the sulking cow and scratched his thinning hair.
'Well it's obvious', says Mulga, *'to rush is not the go.*
To win this contraption's confidence, I'll have to take it slow.'

For weeks he wheeled that cycle 'round when he went out each day.
He even took it into town hitched on behind the dray.
He tried to ride it uphill but the mongrel wouldn't go.
And it always bolted downhill with 'Mulga' screaming *'Whoa!'*

The people in the district had a laugh at poor Bill's plight
But he said the bike was only young and probably would come right.
A bit of careful handling should be all that it would need.
He always carried axle grease to tempt the brute with feed.

One Saturday when 'Mulga' thought the bike was going well
He tied it to the rail outside the Eaglehawk Hotel.
He left a pot of oil there to quench the pushbike's thirst
And bowled into the Public Bar to give the suds a burst.

'Mulga Bill' relaxed and sank some schooners with his mates.
They yarned of cattle, droughts and floods and current shearing rates
But not a murmur passed Bill's lips of things that he could ride.
He'd rather not acknowledge that damn bike tied up outside.

Meanwhile, a cheeky ten year old just up from Sydney town
Staying with a cocky's family who lived out on the Downs,
Saw the young part broken cycle tied to a hitching ring
And looked much more kindly on it than the horses did the thing.

He slipped old 'Mulga's' bowline knot and mounted for the fray.
With a practised twist of handlebars, the cycle flowed away.
His torso cleared the saddle as he got weight in the irons.
Through the town of Eaglehawk that bike went fairly flying.

It threw broadsides 'round the corner. The people stared amazed.
The thing that 'Mulga' couldn't ride was right within their gaze.
A school boy from the city kept the push bike under thrall.
It was not what you'd expect to see in Eaglehawk at all.

Like a cannon ball erupting out the front door of the Pub
'Mulga' bolted with his head high like a cleanskin for the scrub
Screaming *'Someone save that child! He don't know that wicked thing
And the havoc and destruction on his person it can bring!'*

The kid said *'Watch this Mister'* and onto the pedals rose.
The back wheel of the cycle flirted under 'Mulga's' nose.
'Mulga' tried a rugby tackle but he couldn't match the pace
And the fast departing bicycle sprayed gravel in his face.

Poor 'Mulga' sat there in the dirt his jaw around his knees,
His backside sitting squarely in a patch of Bogan fleas.
He saw the thing that beat him mastered by a freckled kid.
Resolution came to William and this is what he did.

He walked towards the young lad and held out his hairy paw
For Bill had never met someone who outrode him before.
And all the town of Eaglehawk, they cheered and clapped with joy
When 'Mulga' gave the cycle to the little city boy.

When the stock are slowly stringing down the winding western creeks
Or ringers yarn 'round campfires 'neath the rugged mountain peaks.
They tell the tale of 'Mulga Bill' that mountain horseman bold
Beaten by the Pushbike Breaker who was only ten years old.

Running Board Mick

He drifted out west in the thirties, wild like the gulf country wind.
Free from constraints of convention, he worked, drank and casually sinned.
Up with the best in the stock camps
when the dust and the danger was thick.
Fought and caroused in the townships.
A son of The Outback was Mick.

Man of the distance and saddle. Twisted hard like a new greenhide rope.
At home on the thundering stockhorse flat out down a rubble strewn slope.
Took hold of the life of a stockman,
with hands that were calloused and quick.
Succumbed to the wiles of the inland,
and the bush wove its spell around Mick.

Rolled with the years and the punches, working and drinking his cheques.
Long months of toil and short revels — the life that a ringer expects.
Lay with the maids of the country.
Taken down by the publicans' tricks.
Enmeshing the man from the stations.
The bequest of the Outback was Mick's.

Slipped down like the lowering bottle, haunted crazed look in his eyes.
Smart man once, now a sad comic figure for others to scorn and despise.
Too dirty to ride with the driver,
and always too prone to be sick.
Rode the steps on the cars of the forties.
They knew him as 'Running Board Mick'.

Any chance for a ride to a Bush Pub, clinging on in the dust to the side.
Filthy, decrepit and bloodshot, the husk of a man who could ride.
The bush chews up men and discards them,
for the bush has no conscience to prick.
Young man, heed the cost of your weakness.
Take a good look at 'Running Board Mick'.

Found out on the roadside one morning. Sad end of a nondescript bum.
Stiffened in death by the spoon drain. Still reeking of vomit and rum.
Who remembers the sun bronzed young centaur,
who dashed where the timber was thick?
Just another drunk dead in the gutter,
will eulogise 'Running Board Mick'.

Bent and Grey

Faded ribbons, tarnished medals, baggy suit and halting gait.
Walking close in case he stumbles means I often stop and wait.
Bowed back and slumping shoulders, reumey eyes and shuffling feet.
He makes his annual pilgrimage once more along the street.

Bent and grey and somehow shrunken, doesn't see or hear too well.
Years ago he served his country in a grim Pacific hell.
Tries to straighten, bugle trumpeting its haunting, sad lament.
A soldier rising from the ruins of an old man, grey and bent.

Noble figure struggling gamely down towards the Cenotaph.
Not one word from any yobbo. Not one comment. Not one laugh.
Look in reverence on a hero and thank God you chance to be
living well in God's own country by old soldiers' courtesy.

With measured tread I move beside him, a trip I make with pride.
Among the veterans who are with us, we remember those who died.
I support a grand, old soldier marching on each Anzac Day.
Humbly walking in the shadow of an old man, bent and grey.

Desmond & the Dunny Cart

(In the days before sewerage schemes or septic tanks, every home had an Outhouse in the back yard. Towns employed a Nightman who took full tins away and left empty ones, during the hours of darkness. The Nightman's vehicle was commonly known as 'The Dunny Cart'.)

When Desmond finished school days and joined the working world,
His aim was to go someplace where he'd meet a lot of girls,
For Desmond carried tickets on himself most people felt.
His mind was firmly centred on concerns below his belt.

He felt life in the city would much better suit his needs
Than vegetating in the country with us Hicks and Hayseeds.
That young man could see no merit in a life out in the sticks.
For him, a sports car, a penthouse and a large array of chicks.

Now Des came back to see us when a year or two had gone,
To show us poor dumb locals how well he was getting on.
I'd say he only came to visit so we all would get to see
The blonde sheila he brought with him, and his shiny new M.G.

In the Pub we eyed the blonde off, quite impressed by Des's luck.
With her miniskirt hiked up her thigh, she sipped her Fluffy Duck.
She cast her eyes around as Desmond paid for high priced grog.
A rich Squatter's son slid in there like a mongrel cattle dog.

Poor Des was trapped up at the Bar. He never had a chance.
The Squatter's son was fairly smooth. He whipped her up to dance,
And while most of us were grinning, young Des looked fairly sick,
As that slimy rich boy did his best to white ant Des's chick

Now it would appear the Squatter's son was doing fairly well,
But country Pubs — they shut at ten. It saved Des by the bell.
He took her arm and fixed the young bloke with an evil glare
And quickly as he could, he got the blonde piece out of there.

'I'll show you 'round the old place' we heard young Desmond say.
He sprayed the Pub with gravel as the M.G. raced away.
They went tearing over Crompton's rise. The headlights lit the trees.
Then the sound of crunching metal floated on the night time breeze.

It was always there on Saturday. It blocked the road in part.
We knew with perfect certainty, they'd hit the Dunny Cart.
None of us saw the accident. The crash was all we heard.
But even if they weren't deceased, they *had* to be interred.

Well we jumped in cars and got there with all possible haste
To see Desmond and his girlfriend sitting waist deep in the waste.
Now a crash into a Night Cart's no place you'd want to be,
But it's much worse if you are sitting in an open topped M.G.

It was a scene you'd imagine as a punishment from Hell.
The night soil oozing everywhere. I can't describe the smell.
Old Ben the Copper cracked us up as he was prone to do
When he said '*Desmond! It looks as if you're really in the poo!*'

The Nightman saw the joke too, for he had no poo on him.
He'd been up a client's driveway carrying another tin.
Des and the girl to put it mildly, were really on the nose
'Till the Fire Department fixed it up with their high pressure hose.

The sheila turned on Desmond and told him just where to go.
She squelched towards the Squatter's son who didn't want to know.
She screamed abuse at everyone while Desmond hung his head
And I don't think I should repeat the words that young girl said.

Des and the girl left separately, and we've seen Des no more,
But we laugh about him all the time, and one thing is for sure,
If you're looking for a yarn session, to help some stories start,
Just make mention of the Legend of Des and the Dunny Cart.

Skiting Johnny

There's laughs in almost anything you care to think about.
In 'most every situation, you'll find humour, there's no doubt.
But the best laugh that I ever had, I almost split me sides,
was the day that skiting Johnny came to teach us how to ride.

When we put the plant together the Mail Truck brought him in
with the annual branding muster almost ready to begin.
We were sorting out the horses there — five for every man
and once skiting Johnny started, his mouth just ran and ran.

He told us in great detail of the things he'd done and seen
but he had that corn fed look as though he wasn't properly weaned.
Mad bulls or fizzy bullocks wouldn't cause John any harm
He'd learned all about cattle on his old man's dairy farm.

He said '*As far as riding horses goes, there's not much I can't do.
I've had experience in the game. I've owned a horse or two.*'
He used to run a riding school. His chest puffed out with pride
as he told us how he'd tamed the nags that no one else could ride.

Now no one who has been around will ever let his pride
overcome his common sense and boast that he can ride.
For hanging 'round the horse paddock on any western run
there'll be a nag to try you out if you reckon you're a gun.

The head stockman muttered on the side '*Hey Bluey. You and Mitch
Go get the spare horses up. Make sure you get The Witch.
Don't let on that she can buck and we'll take down this mug
To show him he's not dealing with some old riding school plug.*'

'*Now Johnny boy, I'm glad to say we've got a horse for you.
This black mare will be just the thing to show what you can do.
We'll hold her while you get aboard. She's somewhat hard to mount,
But to a bloke of your ability, she'll be of small account.*'

His eyes were sliding nervously and his cheek began to twitch,
as seven grinning stockmen legged him up onto The Witch.
They said '*Johnny, are you ready?*' He said '*I s'pose I am.*'
One buck and John went sailing off head first into the sand.

38

The head stockman smiled an evil smirk and said '*Mate you weren't set.*
We'll catch the mare and I'm quite sure you'll beat the mongrel yet.
We've got a chute just over there. We'll put the bitch inside
'cause if you get a decent start, you'll show us how to ride.'

With his nervous fingers pulling at a button on his shirt,
Johnny stared hard at his boot toe that was scuffling up the dirt.
He didn't seem to see a thing except that doodling boot.
Two ringers jammed his Stetson on and marched him towards the chute.

The Witch stared through the rails with a look of pure hate.
Skiting Johnny's limbs were trembling as they pushed him up the gate.
His voice was close to crying as they jammed him in the stool.
He bleated '*Horses weren't like this back at the Riding School!'*

Bluey patted Johnny's back. '*We've got faith in you mate.'*
The Witch rose up into the air when someone threw the gate.
Like some bat from Hell, she flew, red eyed and black as night
with Johnny pulling leather using all his main and might.

It was plain to see that skiting Johnny wasn't going far.
To prize his hands from off the pommel, you'd need a jemmy bar.
A well known part of Stockman's Lore when dust is churning red,
Is — *He who pulls a Monkey Strap, will get stood on his head.*

Dragged out across the horse's mane, he started his hand stand
with nought in contact with the gear but his white knuckled hands.
The Witch was winning all the way and racking up a score
as skiting Johnny got a taste of stockyard dust once more.

Poor Johnny pushed his battered face out of the dusty earth
to see seven crying ringers all doubled up with mirth.
Face all red with childish rage, he cursed us through and through.
The Head Stockman gasped out through his tears '*Now you get on her Blue.'*

Now Blue was pretty handy, light and fast upon his feet.
In a rush of worn old boot soles, he hit the saddle seat.
Johnny howled in his impotent rage, his being quite incensed
as Bluey raised his hat to him while bucking down the fence.

I s'pose we should be sympathetic and you might think us cruel,
but there's never been a ringer born who wouldn't stir a fool.
Though Station horseplay can be rough, its victims tend to learn
that talk is cheap and men's respect is something that you earn.

Murphy's Law for Horsemen

If the lazy old night horse should drop you

    when you weren't taking care as you ought,

Be assured at least half of the station will be on hand

    to witness the sport.

But the day that you ride like Lance Skuthorpe

    on a wild eyed colt in the scrub,

The best you can possibly hope for,

    is to swear it was true in the Pub.

For it seems one of life's contradictions

    for those people who worship the horse —

When you've taken your fair share of busters,

    it becomes just a matter of course

Each time you get dumped by a soft one,

    it will happen adjacent to home,

But the times that you ride like a champion,

    you'll do it afar and alone!

A Cowboy Has to Ride

His name was Randy Barron. His thing was riding bulls,
crashing chute gates etched upon his soul.
Chap leather slapping wild, pumped his cowboy heart brim full.
Clashing bells, hooves pounding made him whole.

At home in smoky bar rooms where a sense of menace hangs
to explode in fists and boots at any time.
He'd waltzed his share of honeys, seen home boys bare their fangs,
as Randy laid it laughing on the line.

Then came a cold dark minstrel picking out a reaper's tune
when he drew a bull no mortal man could ride.
A horn ran through his ribcage on that fateful afternoon.
Arena dust clouds marked where Randy died.

Don't mourn for Randy Barron. He'll never hear you cry.
A life lived hard for all of his todays.
That cowboy lived a dozen lives before he came to die
and who's to say he did it the wrong way.

Free spirit of the rodeo whose time has come to pass.
In dust and violence Randy lived and died.
A blood stain marks the last chute a wild boy climbed at last
to show us true, a cowboy has to ride.

The World's First Horsebreaker

We've heard the tales of horsemen from the Snowies and the west.
Australian riders stand alone up there with the best.
But did you know an Aussie was the first to ride a moke?
It all began with a man named Ug — a prehistoric bloke.

Now Ug was a Neanderthal with a grimly jutting chin,
Arms swinging down below his knees and clad in Wombat skin
When the centre of Australia was full of creeks and trees
Before the mystic Dreamtime of the Aborigines.

The animals all seemed to be much bigger way back then,
And they were pretty hard to catch for puny, little men.
Old Ug got sore and out of breath. He had no time to snooze
Pursuing those Diprotodons and great, big Kangaroos.

Now hunting every waking hour won't qualify as sport.
Ug hardly had the time to eat the things he chased and caught.
Then an idea started forming in his prehistoric brain,
To ride on some fleet footed beast across the rolling plain

So Ug, he sat and thunk and thunk until his head was sore
'Till he came up with an idea no one ever had before.
A pit trap was what he needed, so Ug, he dug and dug
For by the standard of the times, Ug, he was no mug.

Ug surveyed his pit and hoping something would fall in,
He twisted up a green hide rope from Thingadonton skin,
So he could dig a track out, but his captive couldn't flee,
When he put the rope around its neck and tied it to a tree.

For weeks each day he checked the trap hoping against hope
It would contain a candidate for his new bronco rope,
And then one day, Halloo! Hallay! he found it waiting there!
Within the pit there stood, a Neolithic Brumby Mare.

Around her thick and shaggy neck, he let the greenhide fall
Which proves the Yanks did not invent the Lariat at all.
He pulled it tight and snubbed the end up to a handy tree
Then dug a track into the pit to set his captive free.

The hairy Mare did not consider Ug to be her friend
But she could only bolt until she reached the lasso's end.
That caveman made a flying leap and landed on her back.
He hung and rattled like some prehistoric acrobat.

Though it was not a polished ride, I s'pose you'd have to say
First roper and first rider's pretty good in just one day.
Time after time, that wild Mare flung poor Ug to the ground
In that primitive arena with gibbers* lying 'round.

A dozen times a day or more, he tried that horse to ride.
It hinged on who'd last longer — the Mare or old Ug's hide.
He had no time for hunting and his strength was failing fast
While Mrs. Ug and all the Uglettes were flat out cutting grass.

Then one day when our hero leaped aboard the horse once more,
The Brumby didn't pitch and toss the way she had before,
And as the World's first breaker realised he'd had a win,
He bared split lips and broken teeth in a prehistoric grin.

He climbed off and untied the rope he'd fastened to the tree
But while she might be broke to ride, she wasn't broke to lead.
Ug not wanting to lose her, tied the rope around his waist
And tried to urge the Brumby Mare to go some other place.

The horse was ready to oblige beyond his wildest dreams.
She towed Ug face down up the flat and through two rocky streams.
Rocks and sticks they found their way inside his wombat shirt
And every time he tried to scream, his mouth filled up with dirt.

That Neolithic Neddy showed no signs it would tire,
As the world's first horsebreaker got his baptism of fire.
His head bounced off a basalt rock. '*He'd die!*' I hear you say.
But men were born much tougher back in prehistoric days.

The horse pulled up at last when poor Ug wedged between two trees,
And the world's first horsebreaker rose onto his shaking knees.
As through their shaggy forelocks, horse's eyes met those of man
A lasting truce was forged there in this ancient southern land.

So when you ride your pony that your parents bought for you,
Just think how much you owe to Ug who saw the hard yards through.
Think how those pampered equines of the Show Ring and Race Course
Came from a Neolithic Ringer and a prehistoric horse.

* Gibbers: rocks.

She's A Notta so Bad

'*Don't know why you're wasting your time on a starvation block like that*' stated Baxter Purdy, waving a contemptuous arm at the rock and scrub covered hillside that stretched away from his back boundary fence.

'*Thisa land, she's a notta so bad*' grunted Gino, never pausing in his efforts with mattock and crowbar to lever a large rock out of the sandy soil.

'*Only fit for wallaroos and goannas*' said Baxter. '*Why didn't you buy a decent bit of dirt. You'll starve here.*'

'*I no have a too much a money. This a land, she's a notta so bad*' muttered Gino stabbing the bar down the side of the rock.

Gino didn't spare the time to look up but applied himself to the matter of the rock and waved one hand as Purdy slammed the door of his Landrover and drove off with a '*Bye neighbour*' that missed being civil due to the derisive sneer he put into it.

'*Stupid wog*' he muttered as he drove on checking fences and waters on Carrington Downs his big property that ran up against one corner of the failed World War II Soldier Settlement that was rapidly being bought up by Italian migrants.

'*It's like little Italy out there*' he said to his wife as they took lunch on the shaded verandah after his return to the homestead.

'*I hope they'll be good neighbours Baxter dear*' said Muriel Purdy in her cultivated private school accent. '*But one never knows with foreigners, does one? I suppose we'll just have to wait and see.*'

Purdy nodded looking briefly up from that morning's mail which seemed to contain nothing but bills and more bills.

'*At this rate, I'm going to have to make the Daimler last another year*' he thought.

'*What with poor wool prices and bloody station hands getting a wage rise, the whole damned country's going to the dogs.*'

It was about a week later as Baxter drove along his back fence, he noticed the patch Gino had been working on was cleared of rocks and scrub. Gino and another Mediterranean looking man were putting posts in rows along the two acre paddock.

'*What are you building there?*' he asked with genuine curiosity.

'We make a da, how you say it, trellis for da grapes' smiled Gino. 'Maybe four years I give a you some wine.'

'Don't bother much with plonk' said Purdy ungraciously. 'Do you think you'll still be here in three or four years?'

'Oh, I be here all a right' said Gino. 'This a land, she's a notta so bad.'

Time passed and despite himself, Baxter Purdy developed a grudging admiration for his Italian neighbour's capacity for hard work. When he and his men began at daylight to muster sheep, Gino would be tending his vines, clearing more land or working in his newly planted orchard. The only time the Italian was not there, would be when Gino was helping the other migrant families who had bought the failed Soldier Settlement blocks and were turning them into producing orchards and vineyards.

If Gino was not in the field, nine times out of ten, his plump little wife would be, with their two toddlers playing in the shade as she hoed weeds, pruned or picked rocks and sticks off new clearing.

'Those wogs live on the smell of an oil rag Muriel' he told his wife. 'Vegie gardens, rear their own pigs, eat wallabies and they don't seem to give a damn what people think. All they do is work.'

'Well I'm sure that's all very well for Italians dear' said Muriel in her carefully modulated tones, 'But we established families must maintain certain standards and be seen to take part in the social activities of the district. Oh that reminds me Baxter darling, I saw the most beautiful day wear outfit in Fothergills last week. It would be perfect for the spring meeting, and it's a steal at four hundred and sixty dollars.'

Baxter said nothing. Muriel would buy the thing whether he liked it or not, but deep down Purdy knew they were both living beyond their means, and unless woolprices took a mighty jump, Carrington Downs was in trouble.

The seasons came and went as two more years rolled by. Wool prices stayed low and Baxter's situation at the bank was becoming critical. The weight of his position as a prominent run holder weighed heavy on his shoulders as he drove his boundary.

Gino was driving along his side of the fence on a tractor pulling a spray vat with a wide smile and a wave to his neighbour. Landrover and tractor stopped and Baxter greeted this Italian who should have been beneath his dignity, but seemed to be steadily going forward while he slipped as steadily in the opposite direction.

'New tractor Gino' said Baxter. 'Must have cost a bit.'

'My cousin, he mind a my place three months' said Gino with another wide grin. 'I go pour a da concrete for a da new power station. Buy a da tractor. Now

Gino much a work, more vine, more fruit tree, we make a first wine soon. I bring a you some like a I promise. This a land. She's a notta so bad.'

'*Right Gino. I've got to go*' said Baxter as he let in the clutch and drove away wishing he had something to smile about like the genial Italian.

That evening, Baxter braced himself for the worst, and voiced his concerns to his wife. '*We've got to economise Muriel. Take a look at these figures.*' He spoke with no real hope of a positive reaction.

'*You know figures mean nothing to me, Baxter*' said his wife glancing up from her magazine. '*Can't you sell some sheep or something?*'

'*We don't have any to sell Muriel. The surplus lambs and the culls have already gone this season.*'

'*Of course you have Baxter, there's hundreds of them in the paddocks. I'm not blind you know.*'

'*Those are our flocks, dear*' explained Baxter. '*If I sell some of them, we have less lambs and less wool to sell next season. We can't afford a holiday this year. We've got to stop running 'round the country to every social event, and I don't want you to spend any more money without checking with me first. I've got to see the Bank Manager tomorrow, and if we don't stop spending right now, we are going to lose this place.*'

'*Now you listen to me, Baxter Purdy*' snapped Muriel rising to her feet. '*I did not forsake my city lifestyle and marry you to live like one of those wretched Italians. If you cannot provide me with the simple necessities of polite society, I'm leaving.*'

'*You better see what you can make of this accountant's report*' said Baxter throwing a folder on the coffee table. '*I've got too much on my mind to be bothered arguing with anyone except that supercilious young Manager at the Bank. I'm going to bed.*'

'*I'm not enjoying this any more than you are Mr. Purdy*' said the bespectacled young man sitting behind the desk in the manager's office of the Farmers Bank. '*However,*' he stated emphatically steepling his fingers on the neatly arranged desk top, '*If you cannot guarantee us some form of debt reduction in the next two months, the Bank will have no option but to offer Carrington Downs for sale.*'

'*Now see here*' blustered Purdy. '*No young pup just out of school speaks to me like that. The name of Baxter Purdy carries some weight around here, you know.*'

'*Stop it Mr. Purdy. Stop it right now*' said the young manager holding up one hand with the palm facing Baxter as a harder edge crept into his voice. '*The only thing that carries weight here, are these figures in front of me, and you,*

Sir, are in over your head. Two months, Mr. Purdy. Now if you'll excuse me, I have another appointment.'

Baxter Purdy returned to an empty house. Muriel's car and her clothes were gone. The curtains on the French Doors swung in the breeze that blew in over the verandah ruffling the pages of the accountant's report that lay open on the coffee table.

Baxter sat down heavily on the edge of the sofa and looked around the immaculate lounge that still seemed to hold the frigid air of his wife's disapproval. Tears welled up in his eyes and began to roll down his cheeks. He slumped forward and buried his face in his hands as despair washed over him.

He had no idea how long he sat there, but the light was failing when a vehicle pulled up outside. He rose and walked out to see Gino's green J2 Bedford parked in the driveway and his neighbour standing beside it with two green bottles in his hands.

'You remember neighbour? Four years ago, I tell a you I bring a da wine. She's a ready now.'

A frown crossed the Italian's face. *'Wassa matta? You no look a so good.'*

Purdy sunk down on the edge of the veranda and muttered *'Keep your plonk. Wog.'* under his breath.

'Maybe she's a notta so bad Mr. Purdy. We drink a little wine, yes?' Gino said walking over to put his hand on Baxter's shoulder as a huge broken sob ripped out of the grazier's throat and the tears began to flow again as his shoulder shook under the Italian's hand.

For a moment more, Baxter Purdy fought against his prejudices, then his desperate countenance looked up at Gino and the whole story began to pour out. The cars, the clothes, the lifestyle, the falling returns, mounting debt and the loss of the place his great-grandfather had started. He blurted out his despair in an attempt to somehow rid himself of his grief by pouring it out to a man he had barely tolerated in his arrogance and pride.

Baxter paused with an unaccountable lifting of spirit and Gino produced a corkscrew asking *'You gotta some glass?'*

If any of Baxter Purdy's silvertail friends had arrived, they would have been stunned to see him sitting on the edge of the veranda of his elegant homestead sharing a bottle of homemade wine with an Italian migrant who answered his forlorn confessions in broken English.

'My friend' said Gino with a thoughtful expression. *'Maybe I helpa you. I go now. I come back a tomorrow. Maybe she be OK'*

Before the sun slid across the hills in the east next morning, Gino was back. Baxter stumbled out onto the veranda feeling embarrassment at his outpouring of the night before. He was also suffering from a plain old fashioned hangover from the punishing he'd given the rum bottle after Gino left. A sarcastic comment rose and died before it was spoken, and he stood there looking at the Italian.

'*I talk a my family. We like a to buy your back paddock for da grapes*' Gino gabbled in his accented voice. '*She's a face a da north. Good a for da grapes. Your gran daddy, he buy a her. She's a how you say it, other title? You sell a her no worries.*'

A light of hope leaped in Baxter Purdy's eyes. Then he sank down on the veranda edge next to last night's empty wine bottle. '*I don't know Gino. The price of that paddock might hold the Bank off for a while, but it won't fix the problem.*'

'*Why you no grow a da grapes Baxter?*' said Gino. '*You gotta much a land. We build a winery. Sell a much a wine. We buy a grapes from a you.*'

'*Hell, I don't know anything about grapes.*' said Baxter.

'*Bank a man. He think a you don a know much about a sheep either.*' said Gino with a grin.

'*There's not much I can say to that Gino*' Baxter smiled ruefully, '*but I'm broke. I can't start a new venture.*'

'*You gotta money all over da place Baxter. Why you no sell a dis a block. You gotta house. You gotta woolshed on a your other place down a da road. I checka da map. This a block, she two hundred twenty acre. You still gotta plenty land. Sell a big a flash a house. Maybe bank a man buy a him.*' laughed Gino.

Suddenly the lights went on for Baxter Purdy. The need for prestige and position dropped from his shoulders like a discarded coat. '*You're right Gino*' he spoke with a new strength in his voice. Not one of his flash friends was here to help. Only Gino — a bloke he'd written off as an ignorant migrant. He felt he owed an apology for his attitude, and the attitudes of people like him, to this smiling Italian.

'*Come on in Gino. I'll put the kettle on and we can work out the details. I'll ring the land agent and the Bank when they open.*'

The fourth generation grazier died there on Purdy's veranda at ten past six on a bright Australian morning. Baxter Purdy, for the first time in his forty two years, strode through his opulent family home feeling like his own man.

...   .

It was four years later that a slightly worse for wear, seven year old Landrover and an old green J2 Bedford truck met up on a low ridge with a view to the north. Baxter Purdy and his mate Gino Padrone stepped out of their vehicles to gaze across the neatly tended rows of trellised grape vines that stretched away towards the hills in the blue northern haze.

'*Y'know Gino mate?*' said Baxter '*This a land. She's a notta so bad.*'

Country Lady

She wears a woman's mantle with a child's artless grace,
a siren's thrust of shoulder and of thigh.
A smattering of freckles on a young girl's open face
set off by a calm and level eye.

Unconsciously a woman in her natural elegance
walking proud without cosmetic trickery.
A warm and friendly creature, you can tell that at a glance,
with no doubts about her femininity.

She will climb out of a work ute at a rural cattle sale.
You can find her driving tractors in the dust
or steadying the weaners while her partner holds the tail,
handling any job a Country Woman must.

And she'll still remain a woman without a woman's wiles,
in sweat stained shirt and grimy finger nails.
Her sleek suburban sisters could learn something about style
from that Country Lady perched upon the rails.

Death of a Dream

Weather beaten chimney

shrine of dream departed.

Farmer battled grimly

life his father started.

Fire, Bank or weather

taking soul and reason.

One or all together,

finance tied to season.

Sad, forlorn old chimney

over worn foundation.

Reality's harsh whimsy.

Story of a Nation.

Old dream moving over,

modern money spent.

Roaring of a dozer,

falling monument.

G'Day Barman!

G'day Barman! Pot of beer, Mate. I just blew into town.
Been workin' for a drover. Brought a mob of cattle down.
Got a job here breakin' horses. I need a place to stay.
I'll camp here while I work on this old sort I met today.

Now she isn't real pretty — kinda pear shaped. Dodgy head.
But she's got a set of stock yards and a bonzer bloody shed.
All set on fifty acres with a creek flat by the bridge,
Six dams and seven paddocks and a lightly timbered ridge.

Well I know she's fairly ugly, but I need to break those colts.
That shed'd be the place to tighten up the old truck's bolts,
And I reckon with the lights out, she might be sorta fun.
With what I'll save on rent, Mate, I can sure afford the Rum.

I'll take some flowers and chocolates 'round to perpetrate the scam.
I'll tell her that she's lovely like the hypocrite I am.
A few comments on her dress sense and hair, is sure to please.
I'll slide onto the gravy train there, with the greatest ease.

****

G'day Barman! How yer goin'? Haven't seen you since last week.
Pot of beer, Mate. How'm I goin'? Mate! I'm in there flamin' sweet!
I know that down the beach, she wouldn't rate a second look,
But she can make you laugh and holy dooly, can she cook?

I've met a lot of sheilas. I'll meet more before I croak,
But she's the first one you could call an 'Honorary Bloke'.
She don't see life like dolly birds, but from a different slant.
She doesn't seem to worry when you're full and ignorant.

****

G'day Barman! Me skin's crackin'. I'm tonguein' for a beer.
Haven't seen you for a week? Seems more like a flamin' year.
I've been flat out breakin' colts Mate, and workin' on me truck.
When I met that sheila, it began to turn me luck.

Campin' with this sort's turned out a fairly decent lurk.
She feeds me like a fightin' cock. I'm pickin' up some work.
Beats life out on the stock routes bringin' mobs down from above.
It pains me to admit it, Mate, but strike me — *I'm in love!*

****

G'day Barman! How ya goin' Mate? Y' know we've set the date.
I've been so flamin' busy, haven't seen ya much of late.
There's weddin' plans and sheila's talk — a flamin' social whirl!
I'm happy as a sand boy. Things look good for me and Shirl.

She says I've got to meet her Dad. I met her Mum last week.
I hope the old bloke likes me, or the whole show's up the creek.
Anyway, Mate, you're the first cove I met here in this town,
So when we tie the knot, Mate, I'd like you to come around.

What's that you say, old Mate? You say Shirl's asked you to go?
Me and me flamin' big mouth, sorry Mate, I didn't know.
Fair dinkum, I'm a mongrel! Aw Mate, what can I say?
You say you'll have to be there.....
        To give the bride away!!

A Cat's Memo

Pay heed to this general Meiowmo

I issue to all underlings.

If you can't perform well, then please go.

I won't refer twice to these things.

The catering here is abysmal.

Where, pray, is my lobster and crab?

The menu presented is dismal.

My surroundings are gloomy and drab.

Don't bore me with mundane opinions.

I won't stand for 'home brand' in cans.

Please tell me why all of my minions

are a bevy of weak 'also rans'.

My staff seems the ultimate mismatch.

I require more commitment than that.

Please attend to these matters with dispatch.

Director of Works. *Puss E.Cat.*

Ellwood

Me name am Ellwood. I'm a blue dog
An I'll tell you'se wot I do's.
I bites cattle, chases bitches
And loves rollin' in dead roos.

Fightin' dogs am serious business
An chasin' sticks are beaut.
I likes pats, an' feeds, an' Jack the boss
An' ridin' in the ute.

Hippy Dogs

The 'blockies' from the city will live next door no more.
We won't smell marijuana when the wind blows past our door.
No more grubby, naked children being put outside to freeze.
No more bloody Eastern music drifting on the evening breeze.

They've gone back to the city in disillusionment.
Their compensation payout and their dole allowance spent.
The bloke's parents brought a tow truck just the other day
And took the burnt out kombie van and everything away.

Now my old Man's a bowerbird, of scruples quite bereft,
So he snuck across the paddock to find out what was left.
He found half a deck of Tarot cards, a wind chime from Japan
And twenty pounds of Lentils in a rusty garbage can.

Now Dad, he don't waste nothing, so he brought the Lentils home.
When he suggested we eat some, he was strictly on his own.
The old boy called us all a bunch of fussy fairy sods.
Said he wouldn't see it wasted. He'd feed it to the dogs.

They wouldn't eat straight Lentils, so Dad cooked the mongrels up
With some pumpkins and some millrun and last week's killer's guts.
He fed it for a day or two to all our working dogs,
And strike me if I'm lying, they all *quit the bloody job!*

Have you ever seen a pack of dogs turn hippy overnight?
Well I'm here to tell you Mate, it is a most unusual sight.
They didn't bat an eyelid when mobs of sheep were near.
Regarded the whole business with a kind of canine sneer.

Dad's old Border Collie, Ralph, was quite a sight to see
With a fencing wire bangle where his dewclaw used to be.
He was sniffing 'round the rubbish dump and while I could be wrong,
I'm dead certain he was searching for stuff to build a bong.

And Gyp — that good young Kelpie bitch we'd bred to get some pups,
Neglected all her litter once she ate those Lentils up.
Lay down beneath a shade tree for a sleep she didn't need
And left six hungry puppies screaming madly for a feed.

But hippy dogs or not, we had to muster for the rams.
It tends to stuff the profits up if ewes don't have some lambs.
So Dad got Barty and the twins to be his labour force
And said to me, 'We'll take the ute. You go and catch a horse.'

Mum came straight out to help us and Mum's always full of fire,
On the Ag. bike with a Barcoo dog (tin lids on a wire)
Went roaring 'round and shook the rattle at those woolly rumps,
Then 'guts up' in the bull dust when the Ag. bike hit a stump.

The horse that I was riding was one of those touchy ones.
He didn't have a clue just how to make those jumbucks run.
He dropped his head and sent me up there where the air was thin
When I tried to shift those bludgers shaking stones inside a tin.

The ute went charging past. I saw Dad's wobbling double chins.
He was swearing out the window working Barty and the twins,
Abusing kids and sheep and life and mostly hippy dogs,
'Till he tore the old ute's sump off on an old dead log.

Now you just try to muster sheep without our canine mates.
They were hiding in the Mulga and baulking at the gates.
Dad stranded with a broken ute, me and Mum on foot
And Dad so wild, the twins and Barty with the sheep, went bush.

Fair dinkum, we were looking crook. The whole job blown through
When who should turn up but old Ralph, Gyp and the puppies too.
And those two dogs — they went to work like sheep dogs once again
They cleared those woolly mongrels off that Mulga studded plain.

Everything was back to normal. Our dogs off the dole queue,
And no more hippy bludging once they worked those Lentils through.
Though Dad will never live it down, we learned from Gyp and Ralph.
Give hippy food to working dogs, you'll run a lot yourself.

Conservation Blues

She was the green campaigner from the land across the sea
who'd conserved hell out of eagles symbolising liberty.
Her outrage knew no boundaries when she heard the dreadful news
Those unspeakable Australians were culling Kangaroos!

The Government condoned it – claimed it did the place no harm.
By proxy they were blasting figures off their coat of arms!
So she caught a plane to Aussie to set all the creatures free
and liberate the hoppers in the land of Mick Dundee.

She drove into the outback to experience first hand
atrocities committed across Australia's land.
And somewhere west of Roma she saw hordes of Kangaroo
spread all along the bitumen with pigs and emus too.

She pulled up in a small town and descended on the Pub
to investigate these killers inhabiting the scrub.
'It's bad enough you shoot them' she harangued the Public Bar
'But not content with that, it seems you run them down in cars!'

The locals looked her up and down they way bush locals do.
One said *'What? Pull up a Road Train for a flamin' kangaroo?*
Besides it keeps the numbers down' he smirked with twinkling eye
'And if we keep it up, we'll get the last one by and by.'

Old Percy White the Publican who knew a thing or two
had exercised his gift of gab from Perth to Dunnedoo.
He observed that conservationist het up and irate
and girding up his verbal loins, Perc entered the debate.

'You see the road train links the food chain. Keeps the numbers down.
Now indigenous food gatherers only hunt in town.
It maintains a natural balance as everybody knows.
Provides much needed sustenance for kite hawks and for crows.'

She howled *'I don't believe it! Have you no conscience at all?*
I'm aware there's been a count done and still the numbers fall.
What's the outcome of the census? The count of kangaroo?'
Percy answered dead pan *'Ah, I think it's about – two'*

The horror on her outraged face was plain for all to see
in that sudden deathly silence of the stunned variety.
'I pray to God I'm not too late to save the final pair.
I'll take this up in Canberra. I'm heading straight down there.'

She headed for her rental car a Nation's wrath to stir
and never stopped to think old Perc had had a lend of her.
She called upon her zealot's fire this monstrous wrong to right
and gunned the renter southward heading out into the night.

Like a prophet bound for glory, her cause a shining star,
she rode her flaming chariot – a small white rental car –
to save the final breeding pair of Aussie macropods,
when a roo jumped in her headlights, she screamed out '***Oh! My God!***'

'I'm a murderer the breed destroyed! The roo is gone for good!'
as two long legs and a tail disappeared beneath the hood.
Then she halted on the shoulder, the car bogged in the sand,
with a badly shattered vision for fauna of this land.

She stared in desperation through barely focused eyes,
voice mumbling of extinctions and a specie's sad demise.
A truck stopped by the wrecked car in the early morning light.
She was cradling the dead roo's head. Her face a deathly white.

The driver who had found her stooped to catch her whispered plea
'A specie's wiped out totally, and all because of me.'
That sensitive truck driver said *'There's more. It's not too late.*
I got seven in a mob back there by Charlie Wilson's gate.'

Spectres of the Past

A swagman sat in solitude beside his tiny fire
reliving dreams of yesterday before his youth expired.
Half closed eyes snapped open to reflect soft lunar light.
A mellow moon rose toward the stars to wash away the night.

A shiver ran through his old frame. He sat as still as stone
and perceived a sense of unity though achingly alone.
Then all at once he saw them there, a shadowy parade.
The spectres of the past filed by in ghostly cavalcade.

Led by a naked, bearded black with woomera and spears
as faintly the corroboree came drifting down the years.
Deep in thrall of ancient dance to pose and thrust and feint.
Sable skin made skeletal by lines of ochre paint.

Came an old time drover, stockwhip draped around his hand,
a cattleman, Buchanan school, who opened up this land.
Face beneath the cabbage hat deep lined by wind and drought.
His spirit mob of breeders for a new run further out.

Steady tread and shouldered tools of men who scratched for gold
drew the old man to his youth when he saw them as old
Zealots look. Crimea shirt, slouch hat of forty nine.
Lambing flat to Gympie scrub gold pulled them down the line.

Then faintly drifting on the wind, a whip rang soft and clear
with creak of harness muffled by the drum of running gear.
There came a spectral Cobb and Co across the moon's pale face
with tramp of reefing leaders and a groaning thoroughbrace.

He sat in silent wonder as dead years passed him by,
His shearing and his swaggie mates against a moonlit sky.
The storekeeper. The Publican. The trooper and the rest.
Comrades of the huts and camps that dot the endless west.

He yearned towards the next, a face remembered and so dear.
His only love by fever struck half through her eighteenth year.
Small, shy smile and huge dark eyes, that face he loved the best.
He prayed '*God let me follow her*', heart rising in his breast.

He slumped beside that dying fire all done with hurt and fear.
Soul left shell to heed the call that only he could hear.
He shrugged off his unwanted life, earth's harsh existence cast
and joined that phantom retinue. The Spectres of the Past.

Jim

The dust is on the saddle and the gloss is off the spurs.

The Barcoo bridle needs a spot of grease.

Old Dargin's in the paddock with his tail full of burrs.

Rolling fat he lives a life of peace.

A face that's set in sadness sometimes pauses in the door

framed there by the weathered slabs of grey,

for that old bush built stable will feel his tread no more.

Jim heaves a sigh and wheels his chair away.

Rain

It's Four Thirty in the morning. The rain is pouring down.
The grass and gum trees flexing as it soaks the barren ground.
The lovely moisture soaking through the earth to thirsty roots
I wipe the dust and cobwebs off my long unused gumboots.

There have been a thousand poems on this subject — Welcome Rain!
And the poets' Gods must heave a sigh of 'Here we go again'.
But how can a pastoral poet in the bush remain aloof
When he hears that blessed patter of raindrops on the roof?

I hear the steady dripping on the corrugated iron,
My thoughts go drifting backward to the words of John O'Brien
To those lightsome noisesome elves he wrote about in 'Hanrahan'
And flashing roaring storm flood when Anon wrote 'Holy Dan'.

Henry Lawson bought a wee dram from 'Something in Disguise'
When he hung his dripping hat up at 'The Shanty on the Rise'.
Will Ogilvie could not decide if floods or droughts were worse
And Banjo could have used a shower beneath that 'Cloud of Thirst'.

Does another poet really have to lift the pen again
To eulogize in word and verse that hackneyed theme of rain?
Since it's light enough to work now, I think I'll end this rot
For poets should know when to stop, but I hope the rain does not!

Brisbane View

Old sandstone coyly nestled in lea of brooding towers.
Engines drumming, tyres humming constant as the hours.
Cranes like grasping fingers of modern man's unrest.
River tamed and concrete framed, flows turgid from the west.

Prehistoric silhouettes of ancient Bunya Pines.
Towers stark in light and dark, advance in ordered lines.
Muted hues of concrete swiftly crowding out the greens.
Palm and fig survive the dig of ravenous machines.

Remnant scraps of nature left haphazard as by chance.
Man's ideal in block and steel unceasing in advance.
Encapsulated population boxed and packaged neat,
staying sane while there remains one tree across the street.

Crossed up in the Cross

The mustering was finished. Bill made up his mind to go
and head inside to Sydney to see the Royal Show.
A bushman from the plains outback! A likely looking coot!
Twelve stone six and six foot two in his R.M.Williams boots.

He thought *'I'd like to give this Sydney social life a whirl.*
The trouble with the Mulga is it's fairly short of girls.
I'll get meself togged up and give them city Pubs a go.
I haven't lamped a decent sort since Isa Rodeo.'

Bill went walking down the Cross. He hadn't gone too far
when he saw a lit up neon sign that said 'Piano Bar'.
'Aw beauty mate!' the ringer thought. *'Like home in Tagalong.*
We'll stand 'round the goanna and all sing Slim Dusty songs.'

Bill pushed into the dim lit room, but as he stepped inside,
he couldn't see a female there no matter how he tried.
'This Pub's just like the ones outback. This town's a flamin' joke.
I thought I'd find some sheilas here, but all there is, is blokes.'

Bill asked this funny looking bloke *'Will any girls come in?'*
'I hope so mate' the other smirked, *'You see, I'm lesbian.'*
'Pleased to meet ya, Les' said Bill. *'That's real good to know.*
I mustered with a Behan once, but his first name was Joe.'

The Dyke gave Bill a funny look and then had this to say.
'I don't think you quite understand. You see this Bar is gay.'
'Don't look all that gay to me' said Bill with thoughtful face.
'I haven't heard a bloody laugh since I walked in the place.'

He, she, it just rolled its eyes and gazed around the Pub.
Bill thought *'I'm glad you don't meet blokes like that out in the scrub.'*
Then blokey radar kicked right in as slinking from the gloom
long blonde hair and short white skirt came stalking through the room.

She sauntered to the Ladies' Room and then came strolling back,
buttocks meshing gently like two puppies in a sack.
With eyes like red hot rivets, Bill was lusting from afar.
She caught his gaze and winked her eye parading towards the Bar.

Upon the stool right next to Bill she slipped with flashing thigh.
Big green eyes sending signals. Miniskirt hiked way up high.
'*Ah, g'day Darl. Me name is Bill. You've got some classy bits.
Haunches like a well bred mare, and jeez, I like your tits.*'

'*And you can feel them Willie dear.*' Bill thought he would indulge.
He glanced into her lap, and saw a most suspicious bulge.
Bill gasped '*Fair dinkum! Strike me roan! I'd better hit the hoof!
Unless I've got me wires crossed, this sort's a FLAMIN' POOF!*'

Bill bolted from the Bar Room like a piker for the trees
until he felt the muscles in his bum begin to ease.
Slumped panting 'neath a street light fairly trembling in his fright,
fighting down the urge to just run screaming through the night.

A cove with bags beneath his eyes stepped from the busy throng.
He even wore a ringer's hat, but somehow wore it wrong.
Bill thought for a fleeting moment '*Maybe he's True Blue*'
He said '*Dahling, can I help you?*' Bill kept shooting through.

His panic reignited, poor Bill hit the toe again
charging down the bitumen all shiny from the rain.
He started slowing when he saw a taxi up ahead,
a bloke behind the wheel with a bandage 'round his head.

The cabbie sat beside the kerb, his motor idling slow.
'*One thousand greetings Sahib, Sir. Where would you like to go?*'
'*I don't give a stuff mate, just as long as you're not queer.
Gun that flamin' motor and please get me out of here.*'

Bill bolted from the city to the land he loves the best.
He's back home ringing cattle in the Gidyea scented west
where plains merge with the scrub line and a man can touch the sky
and draft the bulls from heifers using nothing but his eye.

Grandpa Does the A.C.T.

When Grandpa went to Canberra to view the seat of power
he thought the public gallery would amuse him by the hour,
but parliament enraged him with the things they said and did.
It seemed to him they acted like a mob of spoilt kids.

Now Grandpa had to find a way to fill his holiday
instead of listening to the drivel our leaders had to say.
He asked some bureaucratic twerp if he knew where to find
an entertaining pastime that would stimulate his mind.

Now we know most public servants can only flap their gobs
and send you on from place to place to justify their jobs.
After seventeen departments the old bloke went to see,
he found himself right back there in the public gallery.

Grandpa was nearly ready to start tearing out his hair.
Again he asked his question to the same twerp loafing there.
'These parliamentary sittings are a death far worse than fate.
Can you tell me where in this burg, can I find some action, mate?'

The twerp he didn't really care if Grandpa lived or died
so he reached into his pocket and grabbed a card inside.
Then that bureaucratic mongrel whose wage our taxes pay
Said *'Here, take this old fellow, and now please go away.'*

The bastion of Government's also the home of sex
because they sell those naughty movies there rated with an X.
The address Grandpa was given by that bureaucratic fool,
led him straight onto the set of porn producer, Ram O'Toole.

When Grandpa walked onto the set, the place was in a storm.
A little bloke with glasses on, was failing to perform.
The Director raged and tore his hair *'Is that what you call size?'*
The little bloke just did a back flip and started telling lies.

'Get out. You're bloody hopeless! Of my God! Send me a star!
Is there not one man in Canberra? I've hunted near and far!'
Ram O'Toole was hopping mad, steam flying out his ears.
The leading lady lit a fag and opened up a beer.

That lady sprawled upon the bed made Grandpa feel quite fresh.
He yelled out *'Ram mate! I'm your man!'* eyes full of naked flesh.
For Grandpa's standards crumpled as that siren lit his flame.
Confronted by a sight like that, I'd probably do the same.

O'Toole said *'Mate! You're hired! You just go with Marcia here.*
She'll give you a nice cup of tea and help you with your gear.'
Now Marcia was a smart girl. She ran continuity.
She slipped ten blue Viagra pills in Grandpa's cup of tea.

The costuming was simple and soon the pills kicked in.
Grandpa strutted through the doorway in nothing but his skin.
The lady stubbed her smoke out and gave a gasp of joy.
'Get over here, you darling. My! Aren't you a great big boy?'

He hit that lady's workbench like a raging mickey bull
and he didn't need the action call hollered by O'Toole.
The king size bed was bucking, bouncing 'round the wooden floor
while O'Toole yelled *'Go you good thing'* and the lady shouted *'More!'*

At first it seemed his staying power would never go away.
The girl was fit and feisty, but you'd have to back the grey
with Grandma full of 'won'ts' he wasn't gonna miss the 'wills'
all pumped up and firing on those damn Viagra pills.

In time the old bloke faded. Well he's eighty three you know.
But I'm awful proud of Grandpa. He sure gave it a go.
He's top dog down in Canberra — wins by a country mile —
where geriatric feebleness will always be in style.

Now Grandpa is a porn star and his masterpiece is found
where they sell those naughty movies manufactured underground.
And dinkum mate, it's worth a look. So take the chance to see
that Grunting Groaning Epic *'Grandpa Does the ACT'.*

Brown's Flat

Little bush flat at the base of the Bunyas where applebox
flowers and currawongs cry.
Rotted old tank stand and ruined workers' gunyas tucked
under a hillside that sweeps to the sky.
Dry grass and weeds cover old cultivation. The fencing gone
pasturing beef cattle now.
Sad old selection now part of a station, watched by an old
crow on a dead ironbark bough.

Sawmill once stood where an old slab's remaining. Last
relic of engine and bullockie's shout.
Riveted seams under steam pressure straining as sturdy
bush children ran laughing about.
Shrilling of saws, rattling mill shakes and squeals as
bullock teams carry the raw timber down
dragging the brake logs, chains locking the spoked wheels. Steep
drop from the forest beneath the hill's crown.

Womenfolk work at the home on the hillside. Boil up the
copper and knead down the dough.
Kids driving down with the draft horse and fork slide
to bring down the smoko to workers below.
Scenes from our past living only in memory, real for a time
then returning to land.
Watcher, the crow, sees what's left from his tree. A few
rotted reminders that shakily stand.

Epitaph

Old friend, it seems your time has come as it must come to all
for life is but a fleeting thing and those who rise, must fall.
So let us pause and hoist a glass, each one that called you friend.
We loved you as a comrade. Now we toast you at the end.

We enjoyed your easy company, admired your sense of style.
Life richer for each one of us who knew you for a while.
We saw the worth in peaceful times. The quiet strength in strife
embroidered in your likeness on the tapestry of life.

Each one of us will cherish thoughts of you who went away
and all of us lost something with the one who left today.
We gather here in tribute to respect a life well run
and raise a parting glass to you whose earthly days are done.

Vale Jimmy Wilson

Jim Wilson was an actual historic figure who operated in the Darling Downs, Granite Belt and Northern Rivers Region of what was then the Colony of New South Wales.

There is no factual evidence to support the story of the Ballandean incident. It is simply a tale that has been handed down the generations in that district. Some historians have credited the naming of 'Wilsons Downfall' with this incident, but this is incorrect. That Wilson was a store keeper from Tenterfield who spelt his name Willson until the Main Roads Department in its wisdom, changed it to the conventional spelling.

Oral history records that Jimmy Wilson did not die in the incident, but four of his gang and a horse perished under police rifles. I beg poetic license to round the poem off with a message. The story is told that Jim fled that conflict and later died violently in the big scrubs of the Clarence River watershed. This would suggest our Jim was something of a rat-bag who bolted leaving his mates to face the music. Perhaps in another time he would have been a politician.

To compare him with the Kellys, John Gilbert or Ben Hall
As an icon of Australia, would hardly do at all.
But Jimmy Wilson could have been a bushranger of note
If he wasn't quite so fond of pouring liquor down his throat.

Jim was flogged at Moreton Bay. His heart turned hard and cold.
He escaped and roamed the border like a highwayman of old.
So here I will recount the tale as it was told to me
About a wasted, miss-spent life and human frailty.

It happened in the mountains to the west of Ballandean.
From a lookout on a hill top a teamster's dray was seen
But when Jim and his companions bailed up the loaded dray,
They failed to see the teamster send his offsider away.

While Jim Wilson and company were gloating o'er the load
Of assorted wines and spirits for a shanty up the road,
The lad was heading southwards standing in his stirrup straps
Riding hard for Tenterfield town to notify the traps.

The policemen came upon them at closing of the day.
The gang lay 'neath the dray bed in an alcoholic haze.
The revellers had raised a tarp to block the mountain breeze
Which let the troopers trap them there with almost foolish ease.

Above the flapping canvas, the inebriated band
Heard the rattle of the carbines, the shout of '*Wilson. Stand!*'
A rifle ball went screaming off the ironwork of the dray
Howling out across the timber in a snarling ricochet.

Jim's mind flashed to the flogger who had turned his heart to stone
Strapped hard against the triangle, his back scourged to the bone.
He squinted at two troopers o'er his waving rifle sight
And tried to work out who to shoot – the left one or the right.

Targets split then merged together before his shaking gun
While drunken Jimmy wondered '*Was there two or only one?*'
The grim avenging troopers stood against the waning light
As wild birds of the bush land flew in panic stricken flight.

Policemen staunch and steady, leaned into their rifle stocks.
Snicking hammers merged with gunfire and clashing of the blocks.
As a wasted life expired in a pointless death that day
The barking of the schneiders blew Jim Wilson's life away.

Aussies died for many causes. Of such things are heroes made
Like martyrs of Eureka in their primitive stockade.
Some Australians died with glory. Others died like dogs.
Jim died in blazing gunfire for a wagon load of grog.

Jim's tale of comic tragedy may make us weep or laugh.
'A victim of our convict past' should be his Epitaph.
A life and death of violence left a message slightly droll.
Why lay one's life aside for nothing more than alcohol?

Come In, Sinner

Constance McAmblin was a devout young woman. This was not surprising considering the fact that her father, the Reverend Hector McAmblin had from the moment of her birth, considered her his personal possession and felt totally justified in demanding her every thought and action be dictated by his divine authority.

In truth, the Reverend McAmblin was little more than a petty tyrant who hid his compulsion to control under a cloak of pious respectability.

Hector filled the post of Minister of the Presbyterian Church in Larkins Corner, a position he had held for thirty years with no hope of promotion. The powers that be in the Church being a lot more aware of Hector's shortcomings than Hector.

The Reverend McAmblin firmly believed he had been invested at birth with a God given right to stick his long and somewhat purplish nose into everybody's business when and where he saw fit. All in the name of God, of course.

Citizens of Larkins Corner regardless of what faith they followed, had become quite used to having their personal and financial affairs rudely probed, and it had become something of a local game to see just how much misinformation they could pump into the pompous Parson.

When Hector dropped into the Toyota Agency to explain to Harry Murphy who ran the place, that only Scottish Presbyterians would find the Kingdom of Heaven, Harry pointed him up the garden path by saying that God had appeared to him in a dream to explain that Catholicism was the only true faith, and the Lord would make his Second Coming driving a Toyota. This led to a denunciation from the pulpit next Sunday of Toyotas as vehicles of Satan. Particularly those driven by Catholics.

Marge Cooper who ran Cooper's dress shop and was a slashing sort in any bloke's eyes, wound him up something shocking when he called in to complain about the hem length of her sole window mannequin. Marge told him she had been approached by the Bishop about starting exotic dance classes in the Anglican Hall to give the church a more 'with it' image.

The sinful lust of the flesh took pride of place that Sunday with particular reference to Henry the Eighth and the heresy of the English Church.

But the one that really got the Reverend Hector going, was the time Merve McCorkindale told him about the nice young man he'd seen talking to Constance.

No one could decide if Merve was the town philosopher who was prone to bouts of drunkenness, or the town drunk who was prone to bouts of philosophy. Somewhere in Merve's past lurked an above average education and he displayed an almost uncanny grasp of the vagaries of human nature.

The Reverend McAmblin accosted Merve as he was taking his daily exercise which consisted of a gentle stroll between Trevor Bidwell's 'Carriers Arms' the top pub, and Mavis Robertson's 'Commercial Inn' the bottom pub. There were only two hotels in Larkins Corner.

Hector had a long standing desire to win Merve back to the fold as his surname suggested Scottish ancestry, but at present, it appeared that the licensed victuallers were well ahead in providing a place of 'worship' for Merve McCorkindale.

Merve was displaying an absorbing interest in two hay aprons and a drenching gun in Taggart and Son's window having seen Hector bearing down on him and wishing at all costs to avoid eye contact with the rampaging Rev.

'Ah Mervyn' he brayed *'I'm pleased I ran into you.'*

Merve resignedly swung 'round to face the loud voice that was better suited to shouting from the pulpit than one on one conversation. Particularly since Hector was one of those people who insisted on standing six inches from their victim's faces and whose words were always accompanied by a fine spray of spittle.

Merve muttered that he vastly preferred conversation to irrigation but the remark sailed straight over the Rev's balding pate, as he launched into his time worn tirade about the evils of drink. Merve practically knew the speech off by heart and had not the slightest intention of heeding the warnings of dire consequences should he fail to commit himself to the bosom of the Church. He waited patiently until Hector stopped to gulp a lungful of air and casually remarked what a fine looking young man he'd seen Constance speaking to in the street yesterday.

'You know, Reverend' said Merve with a malicious twinkle in his eye *'It's a great pleasure to see a young fellow who'se not wearing riding boots and a ringer's hat 'round here for a change.'*

Hector's eyes narrowed and the fanatical gleam faded as the light of suspicion rose in his pale blue orbs.

'Why' grinned Merve *'that leather jacket with the eagle on the back made him look quite like Marlon Brando and his gold ear ring reminded me of the*

gypsies that you never seem to see these days.' 'Yes' he said '*a young bloke like that could certainly turn a girl's head particularly sitting on a big, shiny, chrome plated motor cycle like he was.'*

The Reverend McAmblin seemed to be entering the first stage of apoplexy as Merve winked at him and strolled off towards The Commercial tossing a '*Bye Reverend'* over his shoulder.

Now to be fair to Merve McCorkindale, he'd only been trying to rid himself of a pest and later on he started thinking he may just have let Constance in for some undeserved aggravation from her pious parent.

Merve was on his third pot when the combined editor, reporter, typesetter and general factotum of the Larkins Corner Clarion, Archie Muddleton bustled into the bar. Archie was a small bespectacled bloke who's pockets bulged with pens, pads, handkerchiefs and other accoutrements of the newspaperman's trade. His ink stained fingers drummed on the bar to attract Mavis's attention as he caught Merve's eye and rapped out his usual greeting '*Any news, mate?'*

An idea began taking shape in Merve's head and he said '*Could be Archie. Have one with me'* to give himself time to let the notion develop properly. Mavis poured Archie's usual half rum as Merve pushed a crumpled five dollar note across the bar with a grubby forefinger.

'*So what have you got for me Merve'* said Archie as his drink arrived.

'*Well Archie, I was just thinking how young Constance McAmblin seems to be following the family tradition of providing spiritual succour to misguided sinners.*

I'll tell you what Archie, it was almost inspiring to see the way she was trying to win a young bikie type back to the fold yesterday. I mean Mate, when you think how much trouble she'd be in if her old man caught her talking to someone like that. You'd have to take your hat off to the girl. If I was you, Mate, I'd put something in the paper about it' said Merve with an expression of sincerity on his dial that could have convinced Adolph Hitler to set up a Scholarship for Jewish Students.

Archie Muddleton was nothing if not a newspaperman, and he lived and intended to die by the code that all news is good news. His ink stained fingers began to itch like Mad Dan Morgan's trigger finger as he envisaged the copy flowing from his ancient typewriter that faithfully recorded the life and times of Larkins Corner.

Meanwhile the Reverend Hector had returned home and was dividing his time between fuming and pacing and sometimes both as long as his rather limited application could handle two things at once as he waited for Constance to return from her job at the local hospital.

Constance's footsteps had barely sounded on the manse veranda when Hector's nose appeared 'round the door of the study followed by his face which carried an expression that his daughter had come to recognise as an omen of bad tidings.

'I wish to speak with you, Constance' rang Hector's imperious tones, so Constance walked meekly into the study and seated herself in her parent's presence.

'I understand you were seen talking to some motorcycle riding hooligan in the street yesterday. What do you have to say for yourself, young lady?'

'Oh Daddy' Constance murmured demurely, *'He was simply asking which road he should take to get back on the Highway, and I thought it my Christian duty to offer aid to a traveller. Did I do wrong?'*

Constance had dealt with her father's tirades before, and she had a pretty fair idea how to wheel Hector before he got into full stride. *'I'm sorry Daddy, but you always taught me to offer help when it was asked for. I apologise if I displeased you.'*

This took most of the wind out of Hector's sails, but to keep up appearances, he made Constance sit through twenty minutes of the dangers of associating with ungodly people. The incident would probably have ended there if Archie Muddleton's fertile mind had not been busy making mountains out of molehills – a trait common to journalists in more places than Larkins Corner.

'Like father like daughter' shouted the headline on page two of that week's edition of *The Clarion*. It probably would have made the front page if it hadn't been for Dick Carter taking delivery of a brand new John Deere tractor.

Archie had waxed lyrical about the noble efforts of this young flower of Larkins Corner womanhood carrying on her sire's efforts to bring lost souls back to the bosom of the church.

The Reverend McAmblin spent several thoughtful hours studying the local rag before convincing himself that Archie Muddleton's flowery rhetoric was in fact a sign from above that he, Hector McAmblin had been shown the path of his offspring's calling by Divine Intervention. It was obviously God's will that Constance carry the word to lost souls of the biker brotherhood. It was also unthinkable that Hector's role was nothing more than parent of a prophet, so the Almighty must have intended him to act as Crusade Co-ordinator.

The annual 'Blossom Festival' in Harcourts Range, a fruit growing town on the next watershed, had become something of a rendezvous for the motorcycling fraternity. Next month on the Saturday of the big weekend,

Hector's ancient Morris Oxford rumbled out of town loaded with religious pamphlets and Constance.

In the weeks that followed the McAmblin Crusade for Bikie Betterment in Harcourts Range, people began to notice a certain aura about Constance. Her eyes sparkled. She walked with a spring in her step and people she met simply couldn't help being cheered by the glow of happiness and warmth she radiated. In fact, to anyone slightly more sensitive than Hector, Constance McAmblin was obviously exhibiting all the signs of a woman in love.

It had the local gossips fairly seething with curiosity when she was seen quite regularly talking on the public phone at the Post Office. Then one day, suddenly, she was gone.

It was on a Saturday that a large motorcycle pulled up in the street behind the Church where Muriel Popplewaite who spent a lot of time observing, observed Constance crawling through a gap in the hedge with a small backpack to climb up behind a tall, young, leather clad biker and roar out of town.

It seems the Harcourts Range Crusade had rather different results to those Hector expected and instead of Constance converting the Bikers, they'd converted her.

Nugget Peterson and Donny Gloag were on a fishing trip a year later down on the coast. They stopped at a roadhouse for fuel where a large group of bike riders were having lunch at the tables outside. Someone yelled out *'Here's your burger, Connie'* and Donny looked over from the pumps to see Constance looking decidedly sinful in tight jeans and a leather vest. Her long hair flew in the breeze and an arm that fairly dripped with silver jewellery was draped around the shoulder of a tall, leather clad, young biker.

'I wouldn't mind betting she had a tattoo on her bum too' confided Nugget to Merve McCorkindale in the Top Pub *'But y'know Merve, she looked a bloody sight happier than she ever did at Hector's place.'*

First Touch

Some years had passed since I had faced a wild unbroken horse.
I trained and rode the ones I bred and handled them of course
as baby foals and weanling colts. The way by far, that's best,
but now she stood across the yard, this filly from the west.

While poised for flight, she paced the rails her proud head turned away
while I her mortal enemy, prepared to make my play.
My fingers set the catching loop to do this job I must,
as slow and dead my crippled leg dragged through the stockyard dust.

For if you brave the breaking yard amongst the flying feet
tradition says be fast of foot and also firm of seat.
Yet here was I all broken down, a horseman past his prime,
a thief of equine freedom who must prove it one more time.

I set her running 'round the fence as fast as I was slow
for though my step has lost its spring, my mind holds much I know
of horses and the way they act, so using common sense,
I stood within the round yard's hub and let her run the fence.

The term horseman is freely used and often tossed around
but saddle quiet and bridle wise are spawned upon the ground.
To fight a young unhandled beast's the action of a fool.
In practiced hands the frenzied flight becomes the breaker's tool.

And though that mare was set to run for ever and a day,
in time she came to understand she could not get away.
Negotiation seeming now to her the only hope,
she spun and faced this tormentor who held the catching rope.

Poised to flee, ears sharply pricked, her velvet muzzle stretched.
Essence of a captive thing against the stockyard etched.
With fear filled eyes and shifting hooves, prepared to run or stand,
her questing lips and stretching neck reached out towards my hand.

She drew my scent and lightly lipped the thing her bright eye saw.
A hand up turned with fingers closed, does not appear a claw.
My eyes downcast no menace there, no cold meat eater's stare.
Then with a sigh, the tension left and I had won the mare.

With settling dust on round bleached rails, we stood beneath the sun.
No primal battle won or lost as two minds fused to one.
A filly's partnership with man now well prepared to start
as I became a zone of peace to soothe that wild heart.

Images

Addicted to saddle and bridle,
    to the whistling crack of the fall,
A stockman's hard life without family,
    like a shackle enslaving us all.
Boiling of Quarts by the river
    when the days and the country were hard.
Pounding of hooves from a tough bucking horse
    as the dust floated over the yard.

Soft jangle of spurs in the moonlight
    as on the wild scrubbers we'd creep.
The mad wild dash through the timber
    with the rest of the world asleep.
The feel of a good horse beneath you,
    short coupled, the old station stamp.
A smooth flow of power as he'd work by the hour
    on the face of a cutting out camp.

The glow of the back log at midnight
    and the music of horsebells at night.
Taste of black tea in the morning.
    The first smoke as we'd wait for the light.
Steep hills when we mustered the mountains
    and bailed wild bulls in the bogs
With the mist rolling back from the hilltops,
    the shouts and the clamour of dogs.

Memories as mist on the mountains,
    roll away like the days that are past.
The saddle and bridle are idle.
    The whip and spurs hung up at last.
When I sit by the fire in the evenings
    at peace with my world and my wife,
Then I let those old memories come stealing —
    images of an old ringer's life.

Getting Old

My legs are unreliable. My step has lost its spring.
I try to stand a strainer post, I cannot move the thing.
No more I'll mount a rowdy colt who'll rear and plunge away.
And as for ringing shearing sheds, I guess I've had my day.

I couldn't throw a scrubber bull and tie him in the trees.
How could I match the pace on these old weak and creaking knees?
But I can watch the young blokes. I can even raise a cheer
And skite with all the old blokes as we hoist another beer.

No, I don't mind this getting old. It has its lurks and perks.
You can skite and blow and criticise when you're too old to work.
'Though I cannot dance like Elvis, when all is done and said,
I reckon I've got Elvis beat....'cause I'm not bloody dead!

Roxanne's Wedding Dress

Old Hughy was a miser by the powers that man was mean.
Tighter than a fish's bum and nowhere near as clean.
If a flamin' adder bit him old Hughy wouldn't shout.
He smirked and grinned when cash came in and wept as it went out.

To save some petrol in his car he coasted down each slope.
He didn't wash too often 'cause he hated wasting soap.
He wore his wife out years ago. His children all shot through
fed up with eating pumpkin and fat old barren ewes.

Hughy's daughter Roxanne was a maiden sweet and fair —
the darling of the district and every young bloke there.
They were smitten by her beauty each and every single one
and she fell for Peter Carmody, the local Agent's son.

Roxanne and Peter blossomed as love came into flower.
The girls were all a twitter as they planned the bridal shower
and a dark and dirty bucks' night schemed up by Peter's mates
would be initiated once the lovers set the date.

Now weddings are expensive and as custom would decide,
all the costs would fall on Hughy as Father of the Bride.
But Hughy hoped to organise, if things worked out his way,
a marriage made in heaven where he'd hardly have to pay.

He organised the Parson and the church costs weren't too bad
though the hint of a donation made Hughy fairly sad.
When they talked about the breakfast, young Roxanne gave him hell,
for chops were off the menu and pumpkin was as well.

Peter's mother stuck her oar in and suggested things to Hugh
and Hughy wasn't game enough to tell her what to do.
The cost of buying seafood made old Hughy's knees go weak.
She snorted at the thought of serving yabbies from the creek.

The girls ganged up on Hughy, so he took it on the chin
and rang up for a price to get a catering firm in.
With trembling hands, he took the quote and stared at it aghast
as whistling through his cheque book, Hughy felt an icy blast.

When Peter's father got involved, things went from bad to worse.
It was gunna cost his wool cheque to satisfy the thirst
of half the bloody district there all drinking beer and rum.
and Roxanne didn't have a dress yet – another tidy sum.

The girls were buying bridal books and planning Roxanne's gown.
The more they shrieked and fluttered, the more Hughy's mouth turned down
'till finally he spat it and roared '*I don't want to see
another flamin' magazine. You leave the dress to me!*'

Time went marching by and poor Roxanne got quite uptight.
The nuptials getting closer and no wedding dress in sight.
The op-shops and the Trading Post contained no wedding wear
and bridal stores were too damn dear. Hugh wasn't going there.

Just two weeks before the wedding and every local bloke
was on for Peter's Bucks' Night and the stripper from the smoke
the footy team was importing to entertain the boys.
It was rumored she was skillful with unmentionable toys.

The undresser knew her business. Of all the acts she'd tried,
the one that worked the best, was when she came out as a bride.
It always got 'em going, sweat and whistles running free
would greet her sensual combination of raunch and purity.

The Pubs were nearly empty and the footy club was packed.
That Saturday near every bloke turned out to watch her act.
The lights were dimmed, the music blared and Hugh's eyes opened wide
as strutting through the doorway, came a not so blushing bride.

There was no one watching Hughy while the Femme Fatale disrobed,
He crawled between the tables carefully picking up the clothes.
The music stopped, the boys all drooled, she posed with nothing on
so no one saw where Hughy and the bridal gear had gone.

Roxanne looked a picture as the aisle she walked down
and only lousy Hughy knew the background of the gown
for no other bloke had noticed, and while they might suspect,
it was worth the risk to Hughy 'cause he saved a heavy cheque.

As far as the dress was concerned, old Hughy won the day
and for sure he isn't talking. No way he's game to say.
But somewhere in the city, 'mongst the Clubs and knockin' shops,
There's a snakey stripper wondering what happened to her props.

Battle Mountain

A bastion of rocky cliffs in brooding silhouette.
Restless wind still carries faint old phantoms of the night.
A sense of menace hovers over Battle Mountain yet.
Snarling crags in morning light gleam black as anthracite.
Lone falcon, folding pinions, swoops ruthless from the sky.
One more casual killer in this place of predators,
Captured echoes of the past in wild defiant cry.
Frozen prey awaits the strike. One more death, one more.

Withered bones returning to scattered dust and clay.
Blind gullies, tangled thickets hiding shame of yesteryear.
Spirits of the dead remain, that cannot go away,
Crumbled rotted remnants of woomera and spear.
Warrior shades chew ghostly beards denied eternal peace.
Lubras, piccaninnies, grinning skulls all lifeblood shed.
Remnant strewn hillside, harvest of the black police.
Death ground of the Kalkadoons. Wind sighs *They're dead. They're dead!*

Dawn Parade

The flag is gently stirring in the wafting morning breeze
that ruffles hair above the pensive faces.
Sombre shadowed features lit as light steals through the trees
giving thanks they're free by soldiers graces.

The people of a nation pause to grieve and show respect
to lives laid down preserving liberty,
and thank the ghosts of Anzac for the life we all expect.
Australians at peace and living free.

In history of conflict there has never been a war
any thinking person would call good,
but good men died in thousands on a blood soaked foreign shore
doing what their great hearts felt they should.

Countless caring citizens, each April giving thanks
for freedom into which we all were born.
The Spirits of the Anzacs seem to stand in silent ranks
amongst those early gatherings at dawn.

Warm beds left for dawn chill. Once a year they always rise.
Actions replace words most cannot say.
First light strikes the cenotaph. The Last Post fades and dies.
The faithful congregate each Anzac Day.

The H.G. Panel Van

It was on a balmy Sunday in the morning, kind of late,
When Mark and Polly left for Barrington to see a mate.
Now, Mark, he was a likely lad just 18 years and game,
And Polly was a top bloke though he had a sheila's name.

They were cruising 'round the mountain on their way to see the man
Just listening to the music in Mark's H.G. Panel Van.
Good old Mark, he knew a short cut like any local lad,
So they cut off from the range road down a little tractor pad.

It put them on a back road. He had used the track before,
But they bounced out of the forest to a god 'almighty roar!
For on that twisting little bush road where speed is not the rage,
They found themselves entangled in a rally's Special Stage.

Mark was searching for reverse gear. The leaders swept down hard.
A Renault running second, clipped him on the left hand guard.
His fingers gripped the shifter as his eyes were blazing wild
For Mark, he loved that H.G. as a mother loves her child.

He stabbed it into first as Polly grabbed his head and groaned,
And took off behind the field laying rubber on the road.
For Mark had madness in his eyes as Polly he could see,
And 'round the corner sideways came a fighting mad H.G.

He floored it down the incline shifting smoothly with the stick.
The rear wheels bit the gravel and the dust was surging thick.
Took a Sigma on the inside like a shot out of a gun.
The banks reverberating to a howling One Six One.

Polly heard the valves a-bouncing. Mark's jaw was jutting grim.
The van slammed past a Peugeot and annihilated him.
While Polly grabbed the dashboard with his face a mask of fear,
They sideswiped a Celica with the cheek to come too near.

Came charging up a little hill then cut right through the trees,
The whole thing sliding sideways. Back end flying in the breeze.
Cut a hairpin bend right off. Passed at least a dozen cars.
Found the road again while airborne thanking God for Torsion Bars.

He poked the H.G. down the hill the pedal jammed right through.
Went snaking through the crossing as the leaders came in view.
Mark's lip was curled like Elvis' as he eyed that Renault off
Then the old Van gave a shudder and he heard the engine cough.

But a Holden is a Holden. They'll never let you down.
She backfired, blew the blockage through and powered those wheels around.
Went flying down a little straight and caught the leading two –
A Calais and the Renault – and he slammed the H.G. through.

'Round the corner two abreast like demons going hard,
The H.G. clipped the Renault neatly on the left hand guard.
It threw the driver briefly and to Mark revenge was sweet.
He gained a length 'round the left-hander and beat him through the creek.

And there he saw the finish line just as they topped the rise
The crowd was gaping blankly. Their jaws dropped in surprise.
It weren't no cut down rally car with 'fats' and lumpy cam.
What crossed the line in first place, was an H.G. Panel Van.

The Ringers' Club

Have you ever caught a stirrup on a fresh horse in the morn
    With ears hung out and tail tightly clamped,
When white frost clustered thickly in the first grey light of dawn?
    As you reined him up he sidled and he stamped.
Did you slip into the pigskin and feel the saddle crawl
    As he dropped his head and took the reins away
And if he didn't pelt you, felt the greatest thrill of all
    When you sat tall as he bucked into the day?

Have you run a mob of cleanskins through the timber by the moon
    To the coachers on a bright and starlit night
When the good stockhorse you straddled was waltzing to your tune
    And the cattle dogs were spoiling for the fight?
If you've driven through the night to make a draft or rodeo,
    Pushed up to the bar in some bush pub
And backed your mates regardless when some yahoos had a go,
    You're a paid up member of The Ringers' Club!

Have you battled in the black soil when the old Toyota bogged
    And sweated blood with shovels and the jacks
When the mud was thick and gluey, sticking to you as you flogged
    Your way along those slippery sunken tracks?
Ever seen gaunt dying breeders clutched in talons of the drought?
    Killed the calves to save their mothers and the breed,
Then heart breaking for the shambling wrecks, you nursed them further out
    To the only creek that held a trace of feed?

Have you seen the country blossom when the summer storms arrive
    Changing to a green and verdant place?
Stood there soaking wet and felt the bushland come alive
    And gloried in the rain upon your face?
If you've felt the stinging branches lash across your bloodstained cheeks
    Fighting wild bush cattle from the scrub
As you tossed the racing mickies in the breakaways and creeks,
    Then you're a member of The Ringers' Club!

Have you proudly worn the hat and boots, hallmark of your trade,
 And revelled in the spurs and stockwhip too?
Have you grinned and felt superior to the City's mad parade
 And blued if someone called you 'Jackeroo'?
If you've read Henry and Banjo or sung along with Slim
 When you've put in a day longer than most;
You straightened up at sunset as the light was growing dim
 After hanging off a chainsaw ripping posts.

Can you stand an ironbark strainer or twitch a cobb & co,
 Keep a ute running with fencing wire,
Ride an Agbike, pull a bore, toil from go to whoa,
 Turn out any time to fight a fire?
If you read this verse and puzzle at the terminology,
 Don't understand the lingo of the scrub.
If you try to grasp the sentiment but somehow cannot see.
 You've never been a member of The Ringers' Club.

Alcohol

We hear a lot of propaganda in the media these days

About that demon *alcohol* – its low and evil ways.

And while it may be addictive and dangerous to some,

She'd be a pretty dry existence without a beer or rum.

Now I know that life is earnest, stern, serious and staid,

But if you hang around with wowsers and just drink lemonade,

You'll hear no Champagne popping, no beer kegs foam and fizz,

And 'though your life will not be longer, it'll sure seem like it is!

Imported Beer

Silver Lining

Cruel drought shrouded the country day after desperate day.
The land gripped in its talons like a loathsome bird of prey.
Its spectre crouched across the plain and dusty mountain side.
Charlie watched in mute despair as all his cattle died.

A man who rode the grazing lands, top man at his trade,
who'd found his dream and justified the sacrifice he made.
Tucked below the ranges in this place he'd made his stand
to love his girl and raise his sons there on his own land.

A backward step was not his way. Charlie stood to meet
the wreckage of his shattered dreams scattered at his feet.
This cruel and callous country dragged one more bushman down.
He packed his wife and baby son and made his way to town.

Went to working on construction where concrete castles rise
and stink of city living writes its trademark on the skies.
There Charlie and his lady made their vows to start again
as they banked their city wages, yearning for the sunlit plain.

Fixing steel on a highrise Charlie worked to solve his cares
with the riggers building scaffold fifteen stories in the air.
A young man bolting shackles swinging high above the street
broke a harness and was hanging caught by nothing but his feet.

Charlie raced along the scaffold calling out *'Don't struggle mate.'*
The slightest move would send the young man hurtling to his fate.
A hempen coil lying there gave him a ray of hope.
The hands that threw big mickys tied a quick loop in the rope.

His arm swept out to cast the loop flying true and hard
like thousands he had thrown before in dusty bronco yards.
The sure hand of the stockman headed off an awful joke.
Rope snapped 'round that rigger's waist just as the webbing broke.

Feet braced to take the strain, hard muscles cording in his neck,
Charlie hauled the young man 'till he scrambled to the deck.
The pair of them collapsed there grinning wryly through their sweat.
'That's as close' the young bloke gasped out, *'as I ever want to get.'*

Next evening in the twilight just before the night began,
a sleek Mercedes pulled up outside Charlie's caravan.
A prosperous looking city bloke looked Charlie in the eye
as Flying Foxes winged across the dusky evening sky.

He spoke *'I've come to shake the hand of the man who saved my son
and hand to you a token for the selfless deed you've done.
I've learned a bit about you from enquiries I've made.
I picked up your old property in a rural assets trade.'*

*'You've given back my son to me, so very nearly lost.
A piece of country real estate to me is little cost.
The reason I acquired it was to get around a clause
in the Tax Act. Here's the Deed my friend. From me to you. It's yours.'*

Plastic People

The plastic people are moving by
On any city street.
Buildings tall keeping outlooks small.
They move to the masses' beat.
With corporate ladder rungs by day
And disco floors at night,
They play the game to be all the same
And wrong melts into right.

Their minds are ruled by the pages
Of a glossy magazine.
A wrinkled face is a worse disgrace
Than sins that go unseen.
They live as perpetual strangers
With fear a false world brings
In a land of glass,
    Their lives they pass,
        Devoid of real things.

Super Scooper

In sullen heat of summer, bushfires raged across the land.
Despite heroic volunteers, the blaze was out of hand.
A raging, red eyed monster formidable to see.
A juggernaut responsible for the fate of Bob McGee.

Now Bob was an adventurer of mountain sea and sky.
An amazing twist of fate decreed the way he came to die.
Bob was heading out rock climbing, but the fire grew too near.
He turned back from the ranges and dug out his scuba gear.

Down by Brackers Inlet Bob had launched his rubber raft,
sharpened up his trusty spear gun and checked around the craft.
He mused 'I s'pose the fire gang is where I ought to be.
But that's no fun. I'd rather spear a snapper for me tea.'

Now maybe that was when the fates ordained an awful joke
'cause Bob had ducked out on the duty of a rural bloke.
See Bob was from the city. Didn't carry country blood.
Perhaps he didn't understand the rules of fire and flood.

Each time the claws of flood or fire are spread across the land,
tradition says each able bodied man must lend a hand.
Women, kids and older folk turn out to feed the gangs.
The whole district works together to pull disaster's fangs.

Bob fired up the outboard and cruised off across the bay,
light hearted at the prospect of a laid back diving day.
He dropped the hook, put on his gear and slipped into the sea
searching for a fish or two to grace his plate for tea.

As he finned along the surface, eyes trained into the blue,
he failed to see the shadow as it large and larger grew.
A disturbance in the water. An awsome blast of sound,
and Bob was in a dark place that howled and rocked around.

A hundred possibilities through the mind of poor Bob ran.
Was he trapped inside the beak of a gigantic Pelican?
Could there still be Pterodactyls in some region unexplored?
Or was he Jonah reborn? As the monster sloshed and roared

he swam around the darkened space. He couldn't see at all.
'Till he felt a line of rivets when his fingers touched the wall.
Then revelation came so fast it clutched him like a pain.
'I'm in the bloody Super Scooper. That damn firefighting plane!'

He only had a moment 'till they let the water fall,
so Bob was searching frantically for something on the wall
that he could grab and cling to, to keep himself inside.
Something warm was in his wetsuit as the hopper opened wide.

With a yell of desperation, Bob left the big plane's boot.
'Rather than these bloody air tanks, I should 'a packed a chute!
But how was I to know that I'd be snatched up from the sea?
It's not something you'd plan for. I mean — how would ya be?'

So Bob went into skydive mode towards the smoky pall.
He cast away his tanks to try and slow his rate of fall.
With hands and flippers spread out wide, grabbing at the sky
 he hit terminal velocity, and asked his Maker *'Why*?'

The speed of time slowed down for Bob hurtling through the skies.
Images of his whole life went flashing past his eyes.
I'm sure Bob thought *'Well, this is it! This time I go for broke.'*
I hope he made his peace with God plunging through the smoke.

....

When the Super Scooper beat the fire, some blokes were looking 'round
and were stunned to find the carcass of a diver on the ground.
If Bob was still with us today, I'm sure he would have said
'Some days it simply doesn't pay to get out of your bed!'

It Does Not Compute

Have you ever noticed how some people in the trendy scene
Can never come right out and simply tell you what they mean?
When they speak their Yuppie language, it bores us half to death
And two thirds of all the junk they spout is just a waste of breath.

You can't go to the Doctor now. He's called a Medico.
'Affirmative' and 'negative' replace plain 'yes' and 'no'.
The cat goes to an Animal Physican — not a Vet,
And that's before we broach the mysteries of the Internet!

They talk this modern language born on their computer screens.
If you speak plain old Australian, you're a hoary old 'has been'.
It seems now Email, Software and such words are all the rage
As I'm dragged screaming and kicking into this Computer Age.

It caused me apprehension when they brought one in the house.
I nearly put some Ratsak out to get that bloody Mouse.
Gran thought I was being foul and abused me mate, no risk,
When I asked if Hard Drive when ejected, is a Floppy Disc.

I remember when a menu was a thing that you would read
When you sat down in a Cafe to get yourself a feed.
The writing spoke of steak and eggs and bacon, not Websites.
But Mum would belt you 'round the ear for taking megabites.

I suppose I shouldn't whinge because technology is beaut.
But couldn't they have stopped it once they built the Holden Ute?
Though Trendies find me out of date, and my opinions weak
I can't see good old Aussie 'strine' improved by 'yuppiespeak'.

Kids

Paddy the breaker, the local gun, was riding an iron grey colt
With a mouth like wood and a tendency to either buck or bolt.
He rode past Charlie the rabbiter's house as 'round the chicken coop
Came Charlie's son, a lad of six who was bowling a steel hoop.

In years gone by, to bowl a hoop was a favourite children's trick.
They'd run behind as it rolled along, keeping it straight with a stick.
When times were hard a buggy rim was a treasured toy of course
But a rolling hoop can cause some fun if mixed with a green broke horse.

As the thing came rolling down the road straight for Paddy's colt
The mongrel baulked. Any other time he'd throw up his head and bolt.
Paddy swore and flogged with the reins as he cursed his rotten luck.
Then the hoop rolled under the iron grey colt and the horse began to buck.

The rim caught 'round the colts hind legs and nothing would make it slip,
And the breaker knew he was in a spot that would test his horsemanship.
It belted his leg and wouldn't come loose despite all that grey horse did,
While he glared and swore and ground his teeth at that lousy laughing kid.

In desperation, Paddy leaned over and reached down low from the stool
And as his right hand gripped the iron he cursed himself for a fool.
By a stroke of luck, he wriggled it off and the buggy rim came free
And a better show on a bucking horse no one could hope to see.

His left hand clamped on the bridle reins and his right on the steel band
With a horseman's seat and a will of iron, Paddy brought the colt to hand.
The kid stood there with his stick in his hand, in his eyes an appreciative light
'Gee Mister' he said, *'With a bit of practice, you could ride alright!'*

Footnote: From a story told to me by Barney Belford.

The Electric Collar

They invented a gadget over in the Shakey Isles called an Electric Dog Collar, and a handy piece of gear it was too.

The collar had a battery pack and two terminals that sat against the dog's neck. When the person directing operations, pushed a button on the control unit, it gave the dog a small electric shock.

It couldn't be used to teach a dog to work stock because that's either in the animal or it isn't, but it was alright for knocking out bad habits. It was great for sheep dogs that bit. You could wait until the biter or 'tooth fairy' as we used to call them, had its mouth open, then give it a squirt. Timing is everything when training animals and the collar let you get them at just the right moment. The dog didn't associate the shock with you either, so you were still the good guy.

It was handy for re-lining the brakes of dogs that wouldn't stop on command, and just the ticket for those annoying buggers that bark at night.

I was working for a bloke who bought one and that thing managed to cause one of the best dog fights I ever saw.

Albie was a great, big bloke with a voice like an Angus Bull who had the most unruly pack of dogs it was ever my misfortune to work alongside of. He steadfastly refuted all accepted dog training methods like putting a pup on a long rope to teach it to 'stop' and 'come'.

'Makes 'em mechanical' he'd rant. 'Takes all the natural ability out of 'em. You can control a dog with the power of yer voice' he'd shout at me from a distance of two feet. 'You've gotta train yer voice.'

It seemed to me it was a lot easier on the vocal chords to train your dogs to respond to a whistle or at least a verbal command that didn't need volume approaching a sonic boom, and Albie's hounds seemed to be as unimpressed with his 'Trained Voice' as everyone else was.

Before he let his dogs off the chain in the morning, Albie would have to make sure his Landrover was pointed the way he wanted to go. As soon as that pack of tripehounds saw which way the ute was headed, they'd take off in that direction like a full grown greyhound race. Albie would run them to earth somewhere in the next mile or so and in the back of the vehicle, they'd go. I always put my dogs in after his had done their mad scatter and away we'd go to catch up with the tripehounds.

His Landrover was one of those long wheel base ones with a canvas top and no partition between the front and back. Once we got Albie's dogs aboard, my job as passenger was to quell any uprisings with a piece of poly pipe carried especially for the purpose.

Albie had this big black and white dog called Dick who was a bugger for starting fights and the electric collar was going to be the making of him.

The morning of the great training exercise dawned and Albie strapped the battery powered collar on Dick before he let him off the chain. Once we'd caught up with his mob of canine hooligans about a mile down the river and got them in the back, the lesson was set to start.

The little aerial of the control unit was poking out Albie's window and he waited, thumb poised over the button as he drove.

It wasn't long before Dick took to a dog next to him and Albie pushed the button.

Instead of being suitably chastised and sinking to the ute floor with a surprised yelp, Dick blamed the dog on the other side and promptly flew into him. Dick's teeth were firmly imbedded in his opponent's ear when Albie hit the button again so both dogs got shocked that time and immediately turned on the dogs behind them.

With eleven dogs packed into the back of a Landrover troopie there wasn't a lot of room to manouvre and after Albie hit the button for the third time, the back seat area was a seething mass of snarling, slavering sheepdogs.

Albie slammed the brakes on and as hostilities began to spill over into the front seat, it was rapidly becoming obvious that we would be prudent to vacate the vehicle. We tumbled out the doors with Albie still clutching his precious control unit.

'*I'll fix ya, ya bastards!*' he roared and gave the button a prolonged push that injected random jolts of current into the combatants and only served to sool the dogs on to greater efforts.

'*Stop pushin' that fuckin' button!*' I yelled at my boss in a tactful effort to assist him to the conclusion that perhaps this situation was not an ideal proving ground for the new appliance.

I tore the back flap open and whenever I saw a tail or hind leg poking out of the stoush, I'd grab it and haul the dog outside. Albie put his control unit on the bonnet to give me a hand and gradually some semblance of order was restored despite a few contenders attempting to leap back into the fray like Vikings in the grip of the renowned Berserker Fury.

Apart from a lot of bloody ears plus various punctures and lacerations, the warriors were all relatively unscathed. We loaded them up and continued on our way with Dick running beside the vehicle, Albie having decided that prevention was probably better than cure for the time being.

Albie never tried that little stunt again, but I've got to say the collar did do that pack of his some good. At least when he bellowed across a mountain valley in a voice like a rutting stag, his dogs had the grace to stop and look at him before they continued doing exactly as they liked.

The electric collar certainly had its uses and many doggy delinquents were made true believers and returned to the fold by the simple touch of a button. Isn't technology wonderful?

Unfortunately, the Animal Liberationist mob whose mission in life seems to be stuffing things up for everyone, animals included, got them banned and that was that!

Rubin

They say Rubin's a crazy man. They say he's lost the plot,
that Rubin should be locked away. No doubt his bolt is shot.
But if you see the sunbeams dance like fairies through the trees
where dewdrops shine in spider webs, you'll see what Rubin sees.

His glasses thick like bottle ends, his features rough and coarse,
but I have seen this crazy man approach a brumby horse.
No wild thing fears Rubin only we're too blind to see
the pure soul shining brightly from this human oddity.

They want to lock him in a home and take him from his camp.
It doesn't worry Rubin if his shack is cold and damp.
Rubin's in the best of health although he lives this way,
and who will be the wild things' friend if Rubin's locked away.

Different cultures living in a different time or place
would see Rubin as special, not a society's disgrace.
They'd send their children to him so they could find what lies
within that sloping forehead, behind those peaceful eyes.

The parrots and the possums, butcher birds and wallabies
would miss their comrade, Rubin, sliding wraithlike through the trees.
The fault lies with us humans. Only *we* find Rubin odd
and persecute this different soul touched by the hand of God.

Storm

The timber groans and the wild wind moans
      as it creeps in the sheltered lea,
The rain scuds wild and we stoke the fires
      with the wood of the ironbark tree.
The deadwoods crash and the storm's wild lash
      that howls off the mountain crest
As the ridges heave to the tortured trees,
      a bad wind blows from the west.

When a rage is born in the gods of storm
      who shout from the irate skies
As they scream their spite at the fall of night
      and the debris whirls on high,
The wild things creep to their holes to sleep
      or cower in a grip of fear.
Stark flash of light splits the gathering night.
      The heart of the storm draws near.

The house resounds to a crash of sound
      as the rage wheels overhead
While children shake as the heavens break
      burrowed deep in their beds.
The searching wind tries to creep within
      and slides as a serpent weaves
In an evil crawl of the homestead wall
      seeking under the eaves.

Tall gum tree marked in a blaze of sparks
      spurned in a natural cull.
The old farm dog lies still as a log
      ears flat against his skull.
Both man and beast in a path due east
      in shelter and fear reside.
All life entwined in a void of time
      'till the storm rack's wrath subsides.

Monsoon

There's a whisper in the dry grass. A fragrance drifting forth
As every living creature stops to gaze towards the north.
An expectant air of questing, they catch the scent of rain.
The north land wakes from slumber as the monsoon breaks again.

The drover drives his horses through the creeks and o'er the plain
Pushing hard to beat the storm birds that appear before the rain.
The dark and towering thunderheads loom huge against the sky
As by ridge and flat savannah, he throws the miles by.

From the station house verandah the grazier looks out
At distant rain pall heralding the breaking of the drought.
With thoughts of flushing bullocks, heaves a deep contented sigh.
A jagged bolt of lightning rips apart the northern sky.

He smells the brimstone odour of a lightning riven tree
As sheets of rain come sweeping, driven inland off the sea.
A wild wind blown curtain crossing country in a band
Bringing life and procreation to sere and withered land.

The frogs are croaking madly while the insects chirp and sing
Applauding sullen storm clouds and the feast the rains will bring
The thunder rolls a warning with its hollow boom of sound.
The first drops start to patter on the parched and barren ground.

Amid clarions of angels, Thor's mighty hammer rings
The promise of the soft new life flung on the storm's wild wings.
Trees bending to the fury by the tempest winds beset
Pave the way for grass and flowers at the onset of the wet.

The Saga of the Sexual Saddle

Now Buzzard the Land Agent as a prankster reigned supreme.
He was always sucking someone in with some outrageous scheme.
Anything that Buzzard told you could quite easily be a hoax.
The gullible were easy prey for Buzzard and his jokes.

Buzzard kept a horse or two. He showed and rode and drove.
Was reckoned by the locals as a knowledgeable cove.
There weren't too many bad ones that the Buzzard ever fed.
You could say he knew his way around the equine quadruped.

Two young blokes brought in a saddle the Saddler had on show
To find if it was worth the price, from someone in the know.
They weren't the brightest pair around. They could be classed as thick.
One of them was known as Windy and Windy's mate was Dick.

Like a picture of amazement old Buzzard struck a pose
And staring at the saddle said *'Gawd strewth! It's one of those!'*
He said *'My boys, you've really hit the Jackpot I can see.
I didn't think that one of these was in captivity.'*

*'You see, these are special saddles. They have this strange effect
When they come in contact with a member of the fairer sex.
Through quirks in their construction they fit women like a glove.
If you take a lady riding it will turn her thoughts to love.'*

A strange light rose in Windy's eyes. He swapped looks with his mate
And like a cod with gaping mouth, they took the Buzzard's bait.
Consumed with great impatience to the Bank they had to go.
They left old Buzzard smirking like a killing gallows crow.

They ran back to the Saddler their enthusiasm fired
With passion for the purchase that was mostly lust inspired.
Heads filled up with visions of maidens and their charms
Who were slithering seductively into their eager arms.

Soon the whole town heard about it as often is the case
When something funny happens in a little country place.
The vacant smiles on those boys turned into lustful leers
While old Buzzard and the Saddler chuckled over several beers.

They rang up every girl they knew a riding date to make.
Now they had the secret weapon the drought was sure to break.
But the girls all got together and picked Rosie from the Pub
To accept the invitation for a ride out in the scrub.

And Rosie was a beauty, blonde and shapely, fighting fit.
Her old man was a drover and the girl could ride a bit.
But you couldn't say the same about Windy or his mate.
They'd both have trouble sitting on old Granny's garden gate.

Windy rode around to Rosie's with a smirk upon his face
Leading Dick's mare with the sexual saddle girthed in place.
Over Rosie's nubile form his eyes slid up and down.
She sent the old mare pounding down the back road out of town.

And sweet young Rosie really took poor Windy for a ride.
He never saw the way she went no matter how he tried.
He got back hot and bothered with his clothes torn by the scrub
To find the mare was tied up to the tree behind the Pub.

So Windy and his mate still haven't found a way to score
And are desperate and dateless – the way they were before.
The girls and Rosie all still laugh at Windy getting caught
And Buzzard made a hundred on the saddle that he bought.

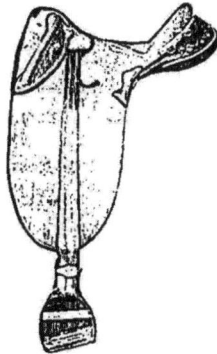

The Teaching Aid

We were sitting 'round a bottle of Bundy Rum one night.
An idea came upon us like a shining, flamin' light.
The best way to teach young riders to keep their tail down
Was a saddle with a buzzer that would make an awful sound.

When they lifted from the pigskin, a squawk it would emit
Which must create embarrassment and cause them soon to sit.
Equestrians would benefit because of tools like these.
Bush boys like us could surely create such technologies.

So Harry hit the saddle shed and tore a stool* apart
While Charlie ratted 'round amongst the ute and Ag Bike parts.
By three o'clock we'd made it with the horn off Dad's old Jag
And a motorcycle battery wired in the saddlebag.

The creation was a beauty. You could switch it off and on
So it only activated when it was sat upon.
We tried it in the round yard. It did everything we said.
Had a rum on the strength of it, and finally went to bed.

Next day, I had to ride the fence along the Eastern side.
It seemed a perfect chance to give that chestnut colt a ride.
Any chance was good enough for him to go to town.
The mongrel took some riding when that Roman nose went down.

I caught him in the darkness. Tied him to a post outside
The saddle shed from which I got my gear to make the ride.
The Rum had made me careless. I must have got it wrong.
I got the saddles mixed and took the prototype along.

Harry had the switch screwed on the off-side saddle pad.
I'd flicked it on unnoticed 'cause my hangover was bad.
Dawn was breaking. I reached a gate at barely half past five.
I eased my weight to step off, and that buzzer came alive.

He froze for half an instant, then he clawed into the air.
A wild grab for the monkey strap* was all that kept me there.
I was half a jump behind him as he rooted down the flat
The buzzer squarking when I lifted, and silent when I sat.

106

I was out behind the saddle looking at a wicked wreck.
I stopped the buzzer briefly as I slithered up his neck.
With that thing squawking madly, there was no way that he'd tire.
If I could turn that Monkey loose, I'd grab that flamin' wire.

And then by accident, my spur got caught up in his flank.
He shoved it up another gear and switched to double rank.
My contact with my steed became as strained as it could be
And damned if that horse didn't turn and jump back under me.

Each time that pony landed, I'd be on his neck or rump.
I didn't know just where he'd go each time he made a jump.
'Though never in control, I was the thing he couldn't heave.
There's just one explanation. I was too damn scared to leave.

Then he bucked over a dam wall pausing at the very brink,
Did a god 'almighty suck back, and dropped me in the drink.
Stirrups flying, buzzer squawking, he left me on my own.
With wet tobacco, boots and pants, I started walking home.

I copped a ragging from my cobbers and loving family.
So Riding School Instructors' jobs are all quite safe from me.
With each Rum inspired brainwave, I just think back to that fall
And Pony Clubbers' bouncing bums don't bother me at all.

---

*   Stool. Slang for saddle.

*   Monkey strap. Leather strap attached to saddle staples on an Australian saddle, used for mounting and as a desperation measure when the rider gets in a 'storm'.

The Sins of the Father

He rolled his swag at seventeen with just one look behind.
Rode away from what had been, and hardened up his mind,
for life was his to make or break, and oh! the world was wide.
Love also his to give and take, and all he took was pride.

With but a longing backward glance, he left his birthing place.
Should understanding flash by chance across that stony face,
But hard lights glittered in Dad's eyes, face set with stubborn pride.
Before the young man's next sunrise, the lad knew he must ride.

He missed his mother's gentle heart, but just the same he ran.
Knowing he and Dad must part, he left the hard old man
and with the same tenacious gene that steered his father's hand,
he left his mark where e'er he'd been across the wide brown land.

By hard work, sweat and acumen, his father's creed he kept.
He faced the worst of beasts and men without a backward step.
Fortune came and pride of place. His lady's heart was won,
a gentle girl, serene of face who birthed and reared his son.

Through joy and tears to teenage years, growing straight and tall
so like his Dad his mother's fears could apprehend the fall.
And sure enough, as manhood grew, two leaders' natures clashed.
As tension rose between the two, a family's hopes were dashed.

His mind refused to compromise. His father's sins unseen.
His child observed through blinded eyes ignoring where he'd been.
Made by the pride that marked his race, to what he was today,
and with a set and stony face, he drove his son away.

Australia's Heroes

Most people in the U.S.A. have heard of Crazy Horse
that Indian folk hero who demolished Custer's force,
Sitting Bull, the Nez Perce Joseph, Cochise, Geronimo.
Indigenous Americans whose deeds of long ago
have brought a blaze of glory to the red man in his land.
But do we heed our native heroes who trod this southern strand?

Britain's sons were gentlemen. Australia's cowardly curs.
Whites who fought were icons while blacks were murderers.
History written by the victor to impress the one who reads
to enhance their reputation and justify their deeds.
We stripped the black man's dignity to brand him as a fool
and cloaked it in a mantle of self-righteous ridicule.

Have you heard of Nemarluck who fought by Kimberley lagoons?
How Beresford was vanquished by the fighting Kalkadoons?
Carbines cracked in Lawn Hill Gorge to still Joe Flick's last hope,
and Jimmy Governor's tragic tale that ended at the rope.
Why don't we as Australians revere our native sons
who fought to save their birthright and died beneath the guns?

A people dispossessed with ease. How could they understand
when born with zero concept of the ownership of land?
Never lost before invasion, they became what they were made.
Once like the lordly squatter, king of all that they surveyed.
So look a little deeper and the truth you'll come to find.
They weren't there for the using, and they had an axe to grind.

It is simple human nature that weak gives way to strong
but pause before you conquer. There's a right way and a wrong.
Consider now the mess we made. What else could we expect?
Can we acknowledge now our failure looking back in retrospect?
Would so much land be sick or saline, devoid of bush and tree
had we consulted them a little when we grabbed its custody?

Must the sins of our forefathers be assigned to you and I?
There's no way to undo history, but we should avoid the lie.
Understanding of our native race can help us live as one
and take away the guilt for things our ancestors have done.
Our Aboriginals were valiant in pursuit of liberty,
human beings guarding culture, just the same as you and me.

He's Saddling Now

Counter lining saddles.
Bench all scarred with knives.
Fixing up the gear to which
Ringers trust their lives.
Grey haired. Nimble fingered.
Hums a tuneless dirge
Feeding in the horsehair,
Sewing down the serge.

Rolled out side of red hide.
Plies the leather plough.
Wet seat leather waiting
Rolled up in a towel.
Worn saddle on the bench top.
Easing out the tacks.
Opening up the staples.
Pulling off the flaps.

Turns the quilting needle.
Gives the thread a pull.
Once he rode a saddle.
Now a saddler's stool.
Squints with satisfaction.
Thread 'round needle flips.
Broken down old stockman.
Gone in knees and hips.

Mind drifting. Fingers working
Wise in saddler's ways.
Dreaming of an outlaw
Back in cattle days.
Sees the red dust churning.
Hears the cheering lads
Spurring up the shoulder
Locked beneath the pads.

Working on the station
For little more than meals.
Beaten up old sandshoes
Replacing Cuban heels.
Sits and smokes at evening.
When his day is done.
Rolls his own Log Cabin.
Doesn't mind a rum.

Young blokes' idle chatter
His sarcasm incurs.
Youngsters' careless confidence.
Leggings, boots and spurs.
Untried and unblooded.
Bragging in their need.
Never rode a bad one
Or swung a wild lead.

Sees the bush land changing.
Roads instead of tracks.
Passing of the packhorse.
Dissipation of the blacks.
Motorbikes and road trains.
Erosion of old ways.
Sitting fixing saddles.
Waiting out his days.

The Regulator

It all began on Saturday down at the bottom Pub.
Big Jake McCrossin came in after months out in the scrub
with a cheque for cutting timber and an urge to knock it down.
So here's the tale of Big Jake's spree that entertained the town.

Jake bowled in the Public Bar intent upon a binge.
Going in he damn near ripped the door right off its hinge.
The locals saw him coming, they all fled to near and far
except old Redback Rasmussen relaxing at the Bar.

Big Jake glared at Redback calmly sipping on a beer.
'I like a bar all to meself, so why are you still here?'
Redback grinned *'Mate I don't do the things I'm told to do
and I don't move for anyone 'cause I can fight. Can you?'*

Big Jake snarled right back at him *'No I can't fight for shit
but any bastard thinks he can, I'll liven up a bit.'*
They stood with furrowed foreheads like two merino rams
flaring nostrils, steely eyes and fists like Xmas hams.

With a swoosh like landing wood ducks, Jake's fist cut through the air.
It reached the spot it aimed for, but old Redback wasn't there.
Then with a sidearm blow that would 'a rung the shed at Louth,
the butt end of a schooner slammed in Jake McCrossin's mouth.

He clamped down like a pig dog spraying blood and broken glass,
then cut loose with a left that knocked old Redback on his arse.
From the hole right under Redback's nose, came an awful roar
and like he was spring loaded, he exploded off the floor.

Toe to toe they slugged it out. Not one would give an inch.
They both soaked up the other's best with no recoil or flinch.
Elbows, knees and blucher boots, foreheads and gouging thumbs.
Gore and blood from biff and thud, teeth snapped off at the gums.

Redback's forehead hit Jake's nose –the old Liverpool Kiss,
then spread it with another slam to prove he didn't miss.
Big Jake was spitting blood and teeth and very nearly beat
till he grabbed old Redback by the cods and swung him off his feet.

What should have been a fearsome roar, came out a strangled squawk
as Redback swung from Big Jake's fist anchored at the fork.
A lesser man would probably have passed out I suppose,
but like a tiger shark, his teeth clamped on Jake's broken nose.

If we'd been selling tickets, man, we would 'a made some coin
to see them two big buggers dancing, joined at nose and groin.
Watchers at the windows made a steady moaning sound.
The more Jake reefed and twisted the more Redback clouted down.

The pair of them burst through the doors and out into the yard
Screaming, swearing, biting, twisting, roaring goin' hard.
Then Mary from behind the bar yelled *'I'll teach ya some sense!'*
and laced into the pair of them with a paling off the fence.

I vowed I'd never give her cheek when Mary cut up mean.
That sheila on her own could flog a flamin' football team.
'cause Mary with a fence batten's as tough as it can get
and she'd stand twice to cast a shadow, about six stone wringin' wet.

That pair of scrappers faced the girl with unbelieving stares.
Just like a foxie standing up two full grown grizzly bears.
Two broken grins split through the haze of bruise and blood and scar
As Mary took an arm of each and led them towards the Bar.

Behind a foaming schooner each, she sat those ratbags down
then through that shattered doorway, filed half the bloody town
to toss their money on the Bar and drink and talk and skite.
We had a howling party the day Mary won the fight.

Big Jake and Redback finished up there drinking side by side
which is just as well or one of them would probably have died.
We all treat Mary with respect. We never tease or bait her
and the batten hangs behind the Bar. It's called 'The Regulator'.

School of the Scrub

I once met a drover who came to our place
With his quick horseman's walk and his leathery face.
A philosopher, poet and home grown sage
With the wisdom he'd learned in an earlier age.
His brother and he both sat down for a drink.
When I looked at the pair it just caused me to think.
Will kids of today be like this in the end,
Or just chasing possessions and money to spend?

People like these from the days that are gone
With the grit and the guts to just keep battling on
In the land where the distance blends into the sky
And the dark scrubs brood over the grim Murranji.
The waters are few and the risks are immense,
Riding five hundred miles with never a fence.
There's no whining or whingeing with people like these.
Just a calm resignation and deep inner peace.

I saw how they'd come by the peace they had found
As they drawled out their yarns and the bottle went 'round.
The tales of the stock routes are grist to my mill.
I've been listening for years and I'm hearing them still.
I said what an honour it seemed to me then
To sit down and drink rum with two Murranji men.
They discounted it gruffly and scoffed in their drinks.
I know it was tougher than anyone thinks.

Now we live in a world of freeways and cars.
Plastic people, weird fashions and dumb movie stars
Where reality fades as the media screams
Out its headlines on TV and smart magazines.
Oh, to ride with the drovers there under the skies
With nothing but distance in front of our eyes.
For the only way out of this civilized push
Is to pack up your traps and go live in the bush.

For the Outback has something for you and for me.
It's not just the place. It's the people you see
From all over the world. They're a knockabout crew
Who are looking for more than just something to do.
There are wild free spirits — some good and some bad,
That most everyday people regard as half mad.
And that's why there's hard cases in each country Pub.
They've all served their time in the School of the Scrub.

Ode to a Ringer

He lay in the dust of the stock yard there.
A strapping fellow with sandy hair.
A short, hard life that had run its course
Smashed on the rails by an outlaw horse.

Just another Ringer – they're everywhere.
They drink too much and they fight and swear.
And townsfolk think that they live too free
For they only see them on the spree.

But did anyone see him on the job
As he swung the lead of a racing mob
And wheeled them back where the scrubs grew tight
In the inky black of an outback night?

Did they see him ride without a care
The wildest horses wearing hair,
The easy grin on his face that sat
As he flogged their shoulders with his hat?

Did they see him stand for the coloured man
Who'd felt the sting of the boss's hand
And take the sack and collect his pay
Then drop the squatter and walk away?

To see his joy at a new felt hat
Or the love of the saddle that he sat.
A simple man with a simple creed.
He was never troubled by power or greed.

So we closed the eyelids upon his face
And left our comrade to God's own grace.
He never squibbed. He had done his best
And our hearts laid our dear old mate to rest.

Uramol

Wally had a hungry block way out past Hogan's Hump.
A stocky bloke with flaming hair we called 'The Blazing Stump'.
Back out in the scrub was where Wal much preferred to live.
A harelip he was born with made him rather sensitive.

The drought had hit him pretty hard. His cattle were in need,
so Wal picked up the telephone to order in some feed.
There was rough graze for mature stock, but Wally's weaner steers
could use a bit of supplement. Molasses and Urea.

The phone girl at the agent's was a vacant headed doll
who dreamed of boys and didn't know the place stocked Uramol.
The supplement Wal needed and the crackling phone line sent
some strange conflicting signals due to Wal's impediment.

'Hullo Sir. May I help you Sir? We'll send out what you need.'
Wal said 'I need Uramol to help stretch out the feed.'
'I'm sorry Sir. I can't make out what your requirements are.'
Wal said 'Stick six blocks of Uramol on the mail car.'

'Six blocks of WHAT? I JUST CAN'T HEAR. This line is rather bad.
I think it's just about the worst connection that I've had.'
You know how redheads fire up, and Wal's patience had flown.
The Blazing Stump roared 'URAMOL!!' down his end of the phone.

She heard that bit alright and screeched 'I'm bloody charging you.
Calling me a moll's a rotten lousy thing to do.
I'll sool the Sergeant onto you, and he's me dad you know!
I'm telling him just what you said you mongrel so and so.'

She slammed down the receiver. Wal thought 'Jees. I've done it now.
I never said she was a moll. The stupid flamin' cow.'
Wal jumped in the Toyota cursing all trademarks and signs,
and made it to the Cop Shop in almost record time.

'Cause Wally wasn't stupid. He realised what he'd said
and to say that to a woman!!…Wal'd rather drop down dead.
The Sergeant stuck his head out and said 'Wal. It's good to see ya.'
Wal blurted in his pumped up state 'Molasses and Urea!'

The cop said '*Wal. You seem upset. I don't sell feed y'know.*
Head down to where me daughter works at Donaghy's & Co.'
A red faced Wal said '*I know that. That's how I come to be here.*
She thought that I'd insulted her but I just asked for Urea.'

The Blazing Stump was fired up from his battle with the 'phone.
As stirry as a Brahma stag locked up all on its own.
In retrospect, you'd have to laugh when poor Wal done his wig
and screamed out '*Getting through to her's like talking sense to pigs.*'

'*What's that you said?*' the Sergeant snarled. His smile overturned.
'*I'll teach you some bloody manners that it seems you never learned.*'
Wal howled '*I don't believe it. Aw Gawd strike me flamin' soul!*
You're not a pig. She's not a tart. I just want **URAMOL***!*'

'*You know! That flamin' supplement you shove down cattle's necks.*
Now I've offended half your family. What else could I expect!
That's why I stay out in the bush. Me speech often annoys.
But just the same, your daughter sure goes through her share of boys.'

'*And you. I've seen you down the Club acting like a hog.*
I've seen better table manners on a flamin' cattle dog.
If you can't cop a critic mate, just crawl back in your hole.
And me! I'm off to Donaghy's to get some Uramol.'

Mix impediments with telephones and foul ups you will see.
The best of cops are known to act like swine occasionally.
When Wal's dilemma comes to mind, all I can say is '*Strewth!*'
And all because a trade name came a bit close to the truth.

Dad's Yarn

There's a story my old man told each Anzac Day
and his audience laughed 'till they cried.
Of two Diggers' wild antics, a theme far away
from the heartache of soldiers who died.
A yarn of two country boys out on The Lair
in Cairo one hot summer's night.
How they broke up a game and each one got a share
and a copper went out like a light.

Now Dick was a Shearer and many a shed
he'd rung in the land of his birth
And Fred was a Ringer no horse, it was said,
could throw, if weight stayed on the girth.
With thousands of others they'd sailed the foam
to jerk Hitler's boys into gear
and make the land safe for the people at home.
'till one night they got on the beer.

Half the night in The Navvie*, then out on the town
the boys spent up most of their pay
with the talk going up and the beer going down.
they drank Cairo dry, so they say.
But as usually happens on sprees such as these
no Spondulie* for more of the same.
So they reckoned they'd ease their financial squeeze
with a bet in a clandestine game.

In a dark dingy alley they found what they sought
by a tallow lamp's guttering light
where the fortunes of soldiers were bartered and bought
in the dead of a black Egypt night.
There were Kiwis and Aussies and Tommies and Jocks
'round a blanket on cobblestones there.
Some were licking their lips, others doing their blocks
as the pennies flew high in the air.

Now our heroes were down to their last lousy bob
and still plagued by a terrible thirst
With the wisdom of drunks, they agreed that the job
was to give the old two-up a burst.
So they laid down their dough to give tails a go
and finance an extension of spree,
when a fat pommie sergeant walked into the show
with an armband that stated MP.

Like ducks on the water or chooks for the chop,
the players just stood there and gaped,
for nine burly troopers were spread out to stop
any chance of a punter's escape.
'Wot's goin' on 'ere?' snarled that mongrel provo
in a voice like the rumble of thunder.
'What's it look like ya mug?' yelled Dick as he rose.
'Here's one for the boys from down under.'

Then Dick he came in with a long looping right
as the sergeant spun 'round with a roar
and the paw that had shore all those sheep tough and tight
landed flush on the bully boy's jaw.
Then that provo lost interest, quite sudden it seemed.
The eyeballs rolled back in his head.
Fred reached in his pocket and suddenly screamed
'Quit it now, or your gunna be dead!'

'Now listen you bastards' Fred growled like a bear
'No guardhouse is gunna see me.
I'll blow meself up and all you too, I swear.
C'mon boys. Just try it and see.'
Then out of his pocket Fred fetched a grenade
and latched onto the pin with his teeth.
He pulled it and spat it as noise seemed to fade
while the sergeant slept on underneath.

For an instant no one up that dark alley stirred,
then they left at a hell of a rate
like nor'wester bullocks that rush at a word
or shorn wethers let out through a gate.
Bolting players and provos were crushed as they clawed
and ran across each other's backs.

Hobnails struck sparks as the cobbles were scored
While Dick and Fred stood in their tracks.

In the blink of an eye that dark alley was bare
as both the boys started to grin.
Fred picked up the pin that was still lying there
and carefully put it back in.
'It's a good job them blokes didn't have time to think.
Still I'm glad that your hand didn't slip'
Said Dick. *'I'd of left here as quick as a wink*
If you'd of let go of the clip.'

You see pulling the pin doesn't fire the rocket.
It's releasing the clip that does that.
So Fred put the hand grenade back in his pocket
and held out his old diggers hat.
Dick scrambled 'round on his knees on the stone
scooping the moola up quick.
Then they left the big sergeant there sleeping alone
before the others woke up to the trick.

Though Dad is long gone, I can still hear him now
as he told that yarn each Anzac day.
How his mates Dick and Fred floored that big pommy cow
With his audience laughing away.
Because none of them talked of the horrors of war
But they'd yarn by the hour of the fun.
Like the night that a Shearer broke one provo's jaw
And a Ringer made all the rest run.

* Navvie: is a slang term for soldiers' licensed or wet canteen.
* Spondulie is slang for 'money'.

Cat With The Condamine Bell

'Whisper' was a holy terror. A true feline to the inch.
Swift and sudden death deliverer to Parrakeet and Finch.
The impact on the fauna was an ugly tale to tell,
So to 'Whisper's' great disgust, she wound up carrying a bell.

A tinkly little bell it was, and 'Whisper's pretty cool.
It'd take more than a thing like that to make her look a fool.
So we added bells accordingly. A second and a third.
And while it cut her down a bit, we still kept losing birds.

So I fired up the forge and made the cat bell of all time.
I cut it from an old handsaw. A FELINE CONDAMINE.
I put a steel ball bearing in to give it lower tone.
For something in a pussy's size, it stood out on its own.

And fair dinkum, it worked perfect. It fixed that cat at last
As our clunking, clonking killer tried to sprint across the grass.
We've belled her with a bullfrog* like a plant horse with the herds,
Now the lizards get a pizzling, but at least we've saved the birds.

*   A Bullfrog is a large deep toned Condamine Bell used on drovers' and stockcamp horses to
enable the horse tailer to locate them in early morning darkness and scrubby country. Different
sized bells were used on selected horses so separate small groups could be located by the sound.
The smallest bell was called a Tinkler and the Bullfrog was the largest. The Condamine Bell got
its name from a Blacksmith located near the Condamine River, who began making bells out of
worn out crosscut saws.

City Fleas

The son of an old mate of Dad's came up to work for us.
He'd come out of the Army and civilian life was tough.
In the forces you will get your pay regardless how you shirk
But the real world, so he found, expected him to work.

He'd had more starts than Phar Lap and failed to make a show
But out of loyalty to Dad's mate, we gave the mug a go.
To be a cattleman, he said, was his great goal in life.
His ute arrived chock full of junk, four dogs and his fat wife.

After one day, all the blokes had had enough of him.
When we got home that evening Mum's face was looking grim.
His wife had let the dogs off and they'd cleaned up all her chooks.
The poor fool's hands were shaking after one of Mum's black looks.

Now Dad, he might have persevered if it hadn't been for Mum
Who fixed him with a glare and said 'You get rid of that bum.'
It must have been the shortest span of someone on our books.
Hell, I'd rather fight Mike Tyson than mess with Mother's chooks.

I can't say we were sorry when he left us the next day
With junk and dogs and missus and a cheque for one day's pay.
No one should have minded losing idiots like these
But the dirty mongrels took their dogs and left their bloody fleas.

Those fleas were flaming killers. You just couldn't make them fall.
They must have been a special strain off street kids in the Mall.
Hard and tough and wiry, you couldn't kill them with a stone.
Those city fleas were so damn tough they had fleas of their own.

We heaped our most vile curses on that bastard and his spouse.
We spread lime around the kennels and underneath the house.
We got bombs and sprays and powders and potions from the Vet
And doused the whole damn station yard, but fleas were breeding yet.

In the wash house in a 'forty four', we mixed a toxic brew
With sheep dip and Asuntol and a jar of Metho too,
And one by one we caught our dogs and dragged them to the brim.
In spite of all their protests, well, we dunked the buggers in.

Fleas bailed off the dogs as we immersed them in the brine
And they pinged like bloody rat shot off the corrugated iron.
Then brandishing a straw broom, Mum ordered us to strip.
Our clothes went in the 'forty four' and we all got a dip.

Then Mum, she started itching, but before her clothes went in
She captured half a dozen fleas and put them in a tin
And I knew next time she went to town, they'd visit Dad's old mate,
Because Mum always gets even instead of just irate.

And finally we beat them. Fought them to the bitter end
Despite the fact those city fleas near drove us 'round the bend.
For Mum, she only settled down when every flea was dead
And she had the cleanest kids and dogs on all the watershed.

Now since the fleas, the hiring has all been done by Mum.
She'll put up with blueing Ringers and blokes who like their Rum
But her employment process is not quite the average sort.
'Please send three current references and a Parasite Report.'

'The Breaker's' Grave

Written to mark the Centenary of The Breaker's execution on 27th February, 1902.

Harry Harbord Morant was young, wild and free,
a warrior poet who made history
laughing his way down the western stock routes,
a rider right down to the spurs on his boots.

Sent out to the southland to work on its runs.
The gentry disposed of its unruly sons
with a ticket one way to a far colony.
'The Breaker' came to us from over the sea.

And history tells us he roamed far and wide.
Though English, he rode as a native could ride.
Steel nerved, firm of seat with the lightest of hands
he earned full respect from the sons of this land.

The century turned full a hundred years past.
The bugle rang out, Harry heeded the blast
as hundreds of young men took ship from our shore
to ride in the Transvaal and battle the Boer.

To this day, the War Office records will state
that 'The Breaker' shot prisoners and sealed his fate.
But Australians know he was killed to disguise
the failure of Generals and cover their lies.

Some day I will go to that far away place
where they buried 'The Breaker' shot down in disgrace.
Pretoria, last rest for one of our sons
who died proud and game under Englishmen's guns.

Perhaps as I stand there his ghost will loom large.
I'll hear his wild yell as the game Walers charge.
And I'll feel a kinship, for this much I know,
a horseman and poet lies sleeping below.

The Fourth Victim

This poem is dedicated to Brian Meldrum, The Tenterfield Saddler, *Nick Bleszynski, author of* Shoot Straight you Bastards, *the Shire Council and people of Tenterfield. It was a moving experience to see JAMES FRANCIS THOMAS given the honour he so richly deserves.*

31.5.2002

We stood among a gathering on the last, crisp day of May
paying homage to a hero and a leader in his day.
A chill New England morning curled the brown grass by the grave
of a caring man, a gentle man, who tried his best to save

a few poor, proud Australians thrown up by fortune's tide,
caught by army intrigue and savaged by their side,
who found old mother England with whom they'd cast their lot,
turned on them like a mongrel dog and calmly had them shot.

And Thomas was a victim too. Fourth of that tragic crew.
The Court Martials left him grieving for the things he could not do.
Sad despair filled up his soul and struck deep in his heart.
James Francis Thomas, Citizen, began to fall apart.

His sad decline reported by the paper he had found.
But the steps of old Frank Thomas are imprinted in the ground
of that small New England border town – a gem among the hills.
The faces of the people showed he was remembered still

as a gentleman who bought a wealth of value to a town.
He took his fellows' troubles on. Morant's case got him down.
He left a splendid citizen. Returned a broken man
To be cast off by society as a run out, also ran.

We stood beside his resting place that final day of May
with thoughts of admiration for this soul who went away.
Had a Wake to toast him. Sang his health in poem and song.
I suppose we rather hoped we all could pass this thought along.

To the spirit of James Francis, may you finally rest in peace
because people recognise you. We can give you this at least.
Your memory is cherished yet. Your reputation healed
and your name is easy on the lips of those in Tenterfield.

Footnote: J.F. Thomas was the Tenterfield Solicitor who defended Harry 'Breaker' Morant and his unfortunate comrades at their Court Martials in South Africa during the Boer War. A remembrance service was held at his graveside on 31st May, 2002 – the centenary of the ending of the South African conflict.

The Phantom Fencer

A tidy little station was the place called *Teamsters Park*.
It was picked up in a ballot by a bloke called Peter Dark.
A bushman and a battler who deserved to own a place.
His experience was written in the lines upon his face.

You win or lose like punting, when you work upon the land,
And luck was not with Peter when that battler made his stand.
A combination of low prices and drought increased his load.
Six years of work went to the Banks and Peter hit the road.

Two Solicitors from Sydney sent the Land Agent a fax
To invest some money long term and minimise their tax.
Their Agent came to view the place. He wasn't very nice.
Claimed the fencing was inadequate to help beat down the price.

Now the fencing on the station had been done by Harry Farr
And a better man than Harry never swung a loaded bar.
He morticed tight and drilled 'em straight as anyone you'd see.
He sunk his strainers four foot plus. His posts went down to three.

He tied off as neat as nine pence and every knot was straight.
It'd sit just where you stopped it when Harry swung a gate.
When he stayed and blocked the angles, they had no chance to shift.
He tied the fence down solid any place that it could lift.

But Harry died one summer in the Pub at Dungaree.
The words upon his tombstone read 'Died from effects of Spree.'
The fraternity of fencers felt their worthy brother's loss.
He willed his gear to Peter Dark — his all time favourite boss.

The Lawyers took delivery. An overseer moved in,
And pretty soon the workers had a low regard for him.
To call himself an Overseer was just a damn disgrace.
He'd be more use on a pig farm than a working cattle place.

Reports came in from people who'd been travelling in the dark.
Weird sightings in the district always close to *Teamsters Park*.
They'd seen Harry's old Land Cruiser infused with an eerie glow
Standing stark on stony ridges only Harry's ghost would know.

One night a sound from outside broke the slumber of the boss
The noise of someone digging underneath the Southern Cross.
Up his spine a spooky chill crept, his peaceful rest to spoil.
The sound of excavation mingled with the smell of soil.

He peered out his bedroom window in the stillness of the night
And saw the Phantom Fencer in the pale moon's eerie light.
A mist of phosphorescence 'round the figure by the hole
As blazing red eyes stared into the overseer's soul.

He heard the chilling noise made by the ghost of Harry Farr,
The scraping of the shovel and the thudding of the bar.
He lay huddled 'neath the blankets a terror stricken wreck,
And prayed to God in Heaven to preserve his worthless neck.

The station workers gathered in the piccaninny dawn.
The boss mumbled incoherently his features pale and drawn.
They saw a fresh dug grave there in the early morning light
And the overseer's hair on end, his face a deathly white.

The overseer rang Sydney and snatched his time that day.
The crew just stood there grinning as the mongrel drove away.
The owners got the agents to find someone for the job
And the staff were quite ecstatic when Darky got the nod.

Harry Farr became a legend in this district's history
Since the Phantom Fencer faded into bush mythology.
People laugh about the ghost that made the overseer scoot
And they wink about the fluoro paint stains on old Peter's ute.

It Was Only Once

Rosco just hated a drink. The first time he snuck down the creek at the ripe old age of thirteen with a bottle of homebrew purloined from his Dad's supply, began his love affair with the bottle.

Whether this enhanced or detracted from his lifestyle, depended on whether the situation was viewed from the perspective of Rosco or almost anybody else. Even dedicated drinkers would have to lean towards the latter because Rosco had never developed much of an understanding of moderation.

He was also one of those blokes who should give liquor a wide berth because he just couldn't handle the stuff. Three drinks and Rosco had the wobbly boot on, but unlike others with no head for grog, he simply would not lie down. As long as someone was awake to annoy, Roscoe would be there making sure they didn't miss out.

They called him 'Rickety Rosco'. At pubs and parties he would lurch from one group to another, butting into conversations by interrupting at a steadily rising volume, until he had their attention, then forgetting what he wanted to say.

Ignoring, insulting, abusing, pushing or punching seemed to have very little effect on him, but away from the booze, he was a top little bloke. Most people handled him by saying that someone at the other end of the room wanted to see him, and he'd immediately stagger off to annoy the unfortunate target he'd been pointed at.

Sober, Rosco was as nice a person and as good a worker as you could wish to see. Drunk, he was an infuriating idiot who could only be silenced by knocking out or dragging away.

Harry Hooker belted him when everyone was drunk at a party one night, and while people all agreed that as usual, Rosco deserved it, Harry still copped a fair bit of flak for being a big enough prick to hammer the poor silly bugger. There really wasn't any defence against a drunk Rosco other than pointing the problem towards someone else. If he'd been objectional or talked 'fight', he would've been fair game, but his inebriated countenance always shone with benevolent goodwill towards whatever unfortunate he had cornered, as the most ridiculous rubbish poured out of his mouth.

Smasher Gibson, the Publican, took pity on him one night and put him to bed in a room at the Pub. In fact, he put him to bed three times because Rosco kept coming back to the Bar until Smasher locked him in by tying the door handle to the verandah rail with a piece of rope.

He even gave him breakfast in the morning and tried to talk a bit of sense into him, but Rosco had never been too keen on listening to well meaning critics. When the previous evening's shortcomings were pointed out to him in the form of comments like *'Jesus you made a prick of yourself last night Rosco'*, his standard, embarrassed, knee jerk reaction was always *'Aw. It was only once'* as he rushed away to avoid further reference to last night's activities.

Smasher, who'd been watching him make a fool of himself every time he came in the Pub for years, was sort of floored by Rosco's parting remark. The Publican's charitable attitude was diminished even more after he discovered a memento Rosco had left him in the bedsheets, that was more suited to disposal in the small room off the end of the verandah.

Antonia Hardesty, first lady of 'Fotherington Park' kicked up a hell of a stink when she waltzed into the ladies toilet adjacent to the member's enclosure on cup day to find Roscoe seated on the floor, lovingly embracing her intended throne.

Rosco was too busy chundering at the time to explain that it was only once, but excuses would have been wasted on Antonia anyway. The shock of almost tripping over a dunny hugging, male drunk in a toilet reserved for females and Members Only Females at that, was just too much.

Antonia had to rush into the only other cubicle to rectify certain blemishes to her immaculate race day costume brought about by surprise and champagne. Presentable once more, she marched out of there with vengeance in her heart and sooled poor old Alec Larkins the Copper, onto the almost unconscious Rosco.

Alex had been handling Rosco and town drunks like him for years. He dragged him out and cleaned him up a bit with a hose, before driving him out to the five mile bridge and leaving him to walk back. Rosco must have endured that sobering stroll a fair few times over the years in spite of his 'only once' protestations.

Luckily for Rosco, young Rodney Hardesty, heir to 'Fotherington Park' and apple of Antonia's eye, managed to make a gold plated arsehole of himself that day as well. Rodney who had been imbibing rather freely with other sons of the silvertail set, decided to demonstrate his prowess with the opposite sex on Leonie Cooper, Smasher Gibson's best looking barmaid. It proved to be a rather embarrassing bum fondling experience for Rodney who got soundly spanked right in front of the members stand, and by a woman at that!

No official action was taken regarding Rodney or Rosco, so Alex Larkins, who was a bush policeman of the old school, more than likely brokered a truce that saved all parties further embarrassment.

They reckon 'leopards don't change their spots' but eventually Rosco got one hell of a fright and put himself on the wagon. It happened when Wilga Wilkinson held a Christmas party with a band and a big bonfire.

Everyone was having a great time drinking and dancing. Rosco was at his rickety best and because of the open air venue, he had ample scope for stumbling. He was in exceptional form and once he began staggering a few steps in any direction, he'd just keep getting faster and faster until he fell over or crashed into someone.

Everybody was making great sport of it as time after time Rosco would veer off his intended line of travel and the crowd would open before him like Moses's Red Sea until gravity took control and he'd spear into the dirt.

A group of teenagers scattered giggling before one of his uncontrolled advances, and Rosco sailed through them and fell headfirst into the fire. Wally Bingham and Julie Kirk grabbed a leg each and hauled him out quick smart. Morrie Cooper extinguished his flaming hair by dumping an esky full of ice and stubbies over his head, and Wilga, being a responsible sort of bloke about fire, had a hose handy that was played over Rosco 'till the ambulance got there.

They carted him off to hospital and due to the quick work of Wally, Julie, Morrie and the rest, there was no serious damage. Rosco was a sore boy for a while all the same, and he had a few interesting new scars to add to his collection.

He must have done a bit of thinking in hospital, and when they let him out, he went straight up to the Pub and asked Smasher not to sell him grog under any circumstances. No one really believed his self-imposed prohibition order would last, but Rosco proved them all wrong.

He'd had a bad fright that night at Wilga's party and there was no doubt Rosco's quality of life and local reputation improved greatly once he knocked off the booze. The saga of Rosco's drinking days came to a quirky end about a week after he came out of hospital.

The no longer 'rickety' Rosco was walking through town when he ran into Alec the copper. Alec looked at him slightly askance and greeted him by saying *'Rosco. You're sober!'*

The old knee jerk reaction kicked in and before he even thought about it, Rosco yelled *'Aw. It was only once,'* and took off up the street.

The Tourist Rush

I've seen some cattle rushes on the ridges and the flats,
And once I saw a rush of cats behind a rush of rats,
But the wildest rush I ever saw I'd really have to say,
Was the time up in the mountains when the Tourists got away.

Old Harry had a trail ride in a little mountain town.
He made a bit of money off them tourists coming 'round.
So Harry got ambitious with the money to be caught.
He advertised for horses and a lot of them he bought.

Bought or borrowed heaps of saddles and gear, old Harry did,
And it must of nearly broke him. It had to cost a quid.
He was ready for the season. He'd really show them how.
Fifty riders on his horses at twenty bucks an hour!!

We were out one day with Harry, just me and young Ted Mack
With fifty head of tourists on a ridge called Whale's Back.
One horse spooked when this goanna ran across a leaning branch.
The lead went off that mountain like a full grown avalanche.

Old Harry rode to block them and he turned the lead horse back,
But the whole mob split behind him on that narrow mountain track.
Still, he almost got the lead wheeled when this hammer-headed bay
Grabbed the bit between his teeth and took that mob away.

We hammered 'round below them on that basalt mountainside.
Banjo's memories would pale beside that terror-stricken ride,
For the man from Snowy River had nothing on us boys,
And Tourists' screaming voices caused a most distracting noise.

Now, Stringybark and saplings would have been a welcome change
From Ti Tree Scrub and Cypress on that rotten basalt range.
There were Tourists racing down the spur as far as we could see,
And only three of us to block them — Old Harry, Ted and me.

We made it to the creek bed and no one would give it best.
Then, spurring up the other side, we rode like men possessed.
With foam flecks flying off the bits, we crossed the second range
As we raked them with the darbys and flogged them with the reins.

Old Harry, he was failing, and I wasn't far behind.
Old blokes like us are getting past hard riding of this kind.
There was no way we could ever have matched the young bloke's speed.
On a dim and distant hillside, we saw young Ted wheel the lead.

Reminiscent of that polo game at Geebung long ago,
Bodies stacked beside the track from go to flamin' whoa,
And only one was topside — a child of the rising sun —
Who said '*Ah so! She Bloody Bonzer! Fair dinkum Aussie fun!*'

Harry's working at the sale yards. He isn't saying much,
And nearly all his inward mail is summonses and such,
And almost all his customers will sue him if they can,
But there's one bright spot for Harry. They just *love* him in Japan.

Bleep! Bleep!

Now Nick, he was a trucker, a deliverer of freight
who earned himself a dollar pushing big rigs interstate.
Kinda rough around the edges, an uncultured sort of bloke.
Called a spade a bleepin' shovel, with no use for trendy folk.

He was heading south to Melbourne, rolling down the inland road.
Practiced feet and fingers nursed the thrusting of the load.
Handling forty tonnes of freighter with the ease you'd drive a car
the diesel pulsing life blood for his faithful Western Star.

The morning light was growing and the night began to fade.
Nick was shifting upwards, rolling down an easy grade.
He saw them in the distance lit up by the morning sun.
A knot of cops and transport men behind a radar gun.

A pimply faced young constable stepped out to flag him down.
There were six rigs on the shoulder, six truckers standing 'round.
Heaps of uniforms were rushing 'round, checking loads and logs.
A handler from the drug squad held his trusty sniffer dog.

Now perhaps Nick's style of greeting was just a trifle strong.
'If you think I'm breakin' any rules, you bleeps are bleepin' wrong.
I've got a bleepin' deadline. I can't stand around all day.
Let's get this bleepin' over. I'll be on me bleepin' way.'

Then up stepped Sergeant Onestone who was quite devoid of tact.
He said 'Listen here you bleephole, I'll aquaint you with the facts.
You can cut your bleepin' swearing, you bleepin' little creep.
You say bleep one more bleepin' time, I'll kick your bleepin' bleep.'

Now Bill who drove for Carlton always packed a video.
He filmed Nick and Sergeant Onestone standing bleeping toe to toe.
A transport man yelled 'Onestone. Shut up and show some sense.
There's a bloke there with a camera gathering evidence.'

Onestone stood there snarling – a most disgruntled man,
he growled 'I suspect narcotics. Kindly open up the pan.'
Nick said 'Mate, don't make me open up that bleepin' door
Or you'll have more bleepin' trouble than you've ever seen before.'

The Sergeant roared '*I order you! Unlock that bleepin' pan.*
This is your last bleepin' warning. I'm not a bluffing man!'
Nick shrugged and swung the door muttering '*Cop it then ya freak.*'
The handler put his dog in with a gruff command to '*Seek.*'

From deep inside the pan there came a low unearthly growl.
A tan flash hit the sniffer who let out a strangled howl.
They landed in a tangle that was spraying blood and fur —
the copper's German Shepherd and a Pit Bull Terrier.

The young cop yelled out '*Stand aside*' and jerked his pistol out.
It wavered all around the place. The two dogs rolled about.
Everybody dived like rabbits beneath the Western Star
as five slugs shot the tyres of the highway patrol car.

The fight was short and brutal and it briefly raged around
then ended with the sniffer lying huddled on the ground.
The handler stood immobile as his face got slowly paler.
The rest of them crawled out from underneath the semitrailer.

Nick said '*Mate. I tried to warn you. You're not too bleepin' bright*
and your mutt should take up dog shows. The bleepin' thing can't fight.
For anything but sniffin' drugs, the mongrel's bleep all use,
and remember mate, you ordered me to turn the Pit Bull loose.'

The Sergeant stomped around the place, eyes bulging like a frog.
Tears rolled down the handler's face as he howled about his dog.
The pimply faced young constable made vows he'd learn to shoot.
The Pit Bull casually cocked its leg and bleeped on Onestone's boot.

A transport man walked up to Nick and said '*We've checked your load.*
Now off you go and catch your dog and head on down the road.'
So Nick did just as he was told. He had no wish to stay,
and leaving chaos in his wake, Nick slowly rolled away.

So have a care policeman, as you swell with righteous pride.
Just take the time to listen. You might see the other side.
Take heed of what's around you. You may discover more,
and don't assume that everyone intends to break the law.

The Buck Runners

We saddled our horses in hours before dawn
in the time when the moon's hanging low.
We'd covered six miles when the night's fleece was shorn
and the range in the east wore a glow.
The sun burst in golden beams over the hill
as its rays chased the shadows away.
We basked in the warmth as it drove off the chill
paying court to a shining new day.

As mountain on mountain ranked proud to the sky
where they faded away in the blue,
wild ranges and sky met in far by and by
in a merging of azure toned hue.
We looked down on the wild mob grazing below
as the cattle dogs scented the breeze.
Keen horses tugged reins as they rose on their toes.
Oh. The glory of mornings like these.

The last shred of mist floated up from the hills
and the brumby foals gambolled at play.
The mares took the lead and the buck whistled shrill.
As whips cracking, we swept to the fray.
With nowhere to run but the valley's defile
hard riders flew guarding the wings,
the sly heelers cramping the stallion's style,
too wise for the hard hooves he slings.

The gravel flew up from the bed of the stream
for an instant to merge with the spray.
The big stallion fought with his mad eyes a'gleam
as the lead mares went racing away.
Young foals running close as if spliced to the flanks
of their mothers, made swifter by fear,
stride for stride never stumbling or breaking their ranks
with the bold stallion guarding the rear.

We hammered and harried them far from their haunts
'till they bowed to the law of the whips.
They trotted, heads lowered, flanks ragged and gaunt
with a weak jaded roll to their hips.
Then up to the yard stripped of all grace and fire
in the glare of the mid morning sun
where a desperate attack by an heroic sire,
sent the buck rolling under the gun.

A day that had started so lovely and proud
seemed so tasteless, now empty and stale.
Though we'd ridden like heroes, I felt like a coward
as they slumped in defeat by the rail.
Their sweat draining down with their souls, to the ground,
I just stood there with nothing to say,
and I felt like a mongrel, a low, rotten hound.
For we'd taken their freedom away.

A Song of the Outback

Skin burnt black by outback sun. Hands light upon the reins.
Look of eagles in his eyes, and red dust in his veins.
He's a symphony of distance, verse of the outside track.
He's flood and fire, as tough as wire, *A Song of the Outback.*

CHORUS

He's a ringer and a singer. He's not like you and me.
A symbol of the building of this Nation's history.
Out in endless distance far from the city's throng.
A ringer and a singer where the man becomes the song.

Hoof beats set the rhythm where wily scrubbers feed.
Stock whips rolling thunder as he swings the flying lead.
A melody of breezes drifting through the black belah
Mingling with the jingling of spur and stirrup bar.

He's echoes in the gorges where the dingo hides her cub.
Cattle lowing softly making music in the scrub.
Gentle carol of the bush land as it ebbs and flows again.
A chorus written for us by the south winds' sad refrain.

A song for all Australians. Why not listen now and then.
Nasal chant at night time 'round the fires of native men.
Murmur of a forest spring where timid creatures go.
Flashing sight of brumbies dashing through the brigalow.

He's the music of the outback and may he always stand
For the special kind of heritage belonging to this land.
The stockman of Australia — an emblem brave and free —
With easy seat, our song complete, rides into history.

Pussycat's Poem

My humans are big and grey headed and they feed me on meat, fish and milk.
I find with some small application, I can tolerate them and their ilk.
I allow them to stroke me and pet me. Condescendingly sleep on their bed
For while I am feral by nature, I'd much rather be warm and well fed.

But those who are little and noisy, I abhor every human like these.
First hint of a malicious midget, sends me out to the rain and the trees.
I remember when I was a kitten and stuck in a house with a brat.
Those tail-tweaking, fur-pulling gremlins have a lasting impact on a cat.

So when they're around, you won't see me. I'll survive on the odd careless mouse.
Until all the children have left here, I'll sulk broodingly under the house.
When I go to pussycat heaven where the rivers and creeks flow with cream,
The presence of undersized goblins simply doesn't fit into my scheme.

When it's time for my spirit to travel to that place where all good pussies go
Where sardines are there for the taking and the mice are arthritic and slow,
Where the humans are hoodwinked by felines, those under five feet are banned,
I'll live as befits my importance in that fabulous childrenless land.

The Day the Cat Got Drunk

A gang of us were sittin' 'round a rum jar out the back
when Snifter had a regular stupidity attack.
He put some home-brewed plonk out with a shot or two of rum
in a bowl of milk for yeller Tom, to give the cat some fun.

Yeller Tom come strollin' 'round and dipped his whiskery mug
to just below the eyeballs, like a wino at the jug,
and started scoffin' spirits like a yob on dollar night.
Then Yeller Tom come up for air and lookin' for a fight.

Poor old 'Bid' the collie who just wouldn't harm a fly
got hammered by a left hook as the mongrel swaggered by.
Bowled straight out to the woodheap on the biggest bloody log,
and started hurling insults at Digger's six pig dogs.

They responded with a bellow and charged him in a pack.
A rum powered yellow tomcat launched a full frontal attack.
He rent them and he smote them with a thousand flashing claws.
I kid you not, that pack had stopped some fairly decent boars.

Of course I'd heard about it, but I'd never seen it done.
One mongrel yellow tomcat made a pack of pig dogs run.
And the bastard was unbearable – struttin' 'round the place
'till them spirits finally hit him, and he fell flat on his face.

Got up and started staggerin'. The old paws wouldn't work.
Reelin' 'round the table like a drunken bloody jerk.
Howlin' out some filthy cat song that sounded pretty rude.
Bounced off a post. Fell down the steps. Crashed on the lawn and spewed.

So we left him out there in the yard sleepin' like a log.
(Best place for a mongrel cat that couldn't hold his grog.)
And later on old Digger, when he went out for a piss,
stuck his head back in and said '*Hey fellas, look at this!*'

And there was poor old Yeller Tom, the bloody drunken slob,
flaked out in a pool of puke with six mice on the job.
And each mouse had a matchstick to flog that blotto cat.
A matchstick to a mouse, is sort 'a like a baseball bat.

We snuck back in and left the mice intent on sweet revenge.
Good job for the cat's sake, Digger's dogs were in the pen.
We laughed about rough justice and it made the rum taste nice.
A cat who flogged six pig dogs, getting done over by mice.

There's no moral to this story, but asked to take a guess,
I'd probably say this warns us about drinkin' to excess.
But I've never seen a drunk take advice when full of brew
and rodents armed with thrashing sticks, are handy in a blue.

I've seen a parrot blind on scotch and two pups full of wine,
and once we got a horse pissed in a camp at Narromine.
Most animals are happy drunks, staggerers, then dreamers.
But don't give grog to cats because *they're bloody two pot screamers!*

Friday Night Lady

A Friday night lady
who's everyone's baby
will never be waltzed to the stars.
Those found in Nightclubs
seldom make life's loves.
You don't find good partners in bars.

Brief pleasure she steals.
Tight dress and high heels.
Strutting her stuff 'neath the strobe.
She's got suitors to spare
but she wears her despair
draped over her life like a robe.

Fake smile can't disguise
hurt in those sad eyes.
Yet each night she's drawn to the flame
of dim lights and false fun
to search for the right one.
Each one of them playing their game.

Lights flash and spin 'round
the band pounds its hard sound.
While hunters are cruising like sharks
all seeking a live one
to give them a night's fun
they cynically pick out their marks.

she'll wake in the dawning
on Saturday morning
to slip from one more stranger's bed.
The guilt that she's feeling
as downstairs she's stealing,
brings back the words her mother said.

'Cause a Friday night lady
whose everyone's baby
will never be waltzed to the stars.
Those found in Nightclubs
Seldom make life's loves.
You won't find good partners in bars.

Sydney or the Bush

Harry was a desert man from out the back of Bourke
And all he'd known in his life, was heat and dust and work.
He didn't blow cheques with his mates or go out on the spree
And was rather fond of saying 'Sydney or the bush for me!'

Thirty seven miles of dingo fence was finally cut out
The gang sat 'round a box of beer and drank the boss's shout.
The boss said 'Harry here's your cheque' and handed him his pay
And Harry said 'I think it's time I had a holiday!'

'Sydney or the bush' had always been old Harry's boast.
He slung his swag into the ute and headed for the coast.
He hummed a tune and drove towards the country 'further in'
While his fingers tapped the rhythm on his old tobacco tin.

The traffic down in Sydney nearly drove him to the Pub.
Quite intimidating for a bloke out of the scrub.
He said 'I've wheeled bullocks on a night camp all alone.
If I can't face Sydney traffic, I should 'a stayed at home.'

Old Harry thought that Bondi Beach was just the place to be
For he was born a desert man. He'd never seen the sea.
Those stories of the ocean he'd heard other people say
Made him long to see the pounding surf in Bondi Bay.

Harry left his room and climbed into the driver's seat.
He made it through the city turning off on Oxford Street.
Swung right at Bondi Junction, then the old ute let him down.
He heard the brake line fracture with a nasty hissing sound.

The broken brake line jammed the throttle linkage open wide.
Harry tried to switch it off and coast into the side
But luck was not with Harry on that cloudless Sydney day.
The key snapped off and then the old ute bolted clean away.

Flying down that Bondi Hill the red lights flashing by,
His bluchers braced against the floor, he aimed for sea and sky.
Harry's brow was sweating hard. His bowels clenched tight with fear
As the passenger side mirror slapped a fat policeman's ear.

He swung the wheel to the right to dodge a semi trailer.
Tore clothing off a gothic chick and turned her three shades paler.
They approached a big left hander, pedestrians in a funk.
Sliced the briefcase off a Mormon and the ear rings off a punk.

The throttle stuck wide open. Harry couldn't shut the power.
The ute howled past the Astra Pub at ninety miles an hour.
Cleaned up some drunken Kiwis, a dealer selling speed,
And a poor old Hare Krishna pigging out on pumpkin seeds.

It went straight over a palm tree and filled the back with fronds.
The bumper ripped a tie-dyed skirt right off a spunky blonde.
The steering wheel nearly crushed by Harry's trembling hands
Went hurtling off the sea wall and took off across the sands.

With tits and towels and transistors all flashing past his eyes,
A hooker touting business and an old bloke selling pies.
Life guards and bikini girls all lining up to see
The old ute join the blind mullets and plunge into the sea.

Flying through the shallows Harry clipped some posing fags
And law abiding bloke he was, went right between the flags.
A life guard blew his whistle. God knows what good that would do.
The old ute lost impulsion as the sea got deep and blue.

It's hard to stop a desert man from out the back of Bourke.
The Pacific took a flogging when Harry went to work.
A body builder had to swim like Olympians do.
Harry missed him but I'll bet he pumped a wing of steroids through.

The ute stopped in the breakers when the wheels left the sand
But looked as if it was prepared to float to Kiwi land.
With Harry at the end of his most terrifying track.
A surfie on the bonnet and a big shark in the back.

He sat up on the window sill. The ute began to sink
And saw the trail of chaos from his trip into the drink.
Squad cars on the esplanade. Policemen issued forth.
So Harry slipped his bluchers off and started swimming north.

He free styled 'round Ben Buckler Point and up past Dover Heights
Then kept flogging through the water 'till South Head came in sight.
And when all poor Harry's energy was very nearly used,
He got caught up by the tide landing somewhere near Vaucluse.

Some trendies at a Soiree didn't quite know what to think
When they saw a sodden Bushie come crawling from the drink.
He made it to his Hotel room by paths mostly unknown,
Grabbed his swag and bolted for the bus station and home.

So if you ever find yourself way out the back of Bourke
You may see some desert men who've just cut out some work.
You'll find old Harry in the lead of that grog swilling push
But he'll never mention Sydney and he'll never leave the bush.

Barny

I put in a bit of time in the back country of New Zealand, and it was there I ran into Barny — a horse with a personality all his own.

It gets pretty cold in the mountains there, with a fair bit of ice and snow. Before all the high country grazing leases were closed down, they mustered all the sheep off the high mountains in autumn and kept them down on the lower country until it snowed. The snow formed a natural boundary and the sheep couldn't get back up on the tops again 'till the spring melt.

While you waited for the snow, you had to keep a pretty close eye on them to keep them down on the flats. Dick Kelly and I were camped out boundary riding a block that ran right back to the main range. We finished our 'hunting down' as they called it, by about two o'clock most days, so it was an easy job and we had a bit of time on our hands.

Horses are well known for being herd animals whose natural defence revolves 'round 'safety in numbers'. However, nobody had bothered to tell Barny about all his deep seated instincts, and he lived out there quite happily all on his own like a sort of horse hermit. The reason Barny was alone, was that he'd worked out early in life that those who don't enter the yards, don't enter the workforce. He'd broken for the high ridges as a weanling the first time they tried to muster him and no one had been able to yard him since.

He probably should have been shot because a twelve year old, unbroken, bush bred stallion could not be regarded as an asset by even the most charitably minded run holder. It seemed that nobody wanted to be the one to use the rifle and after a few years, Barny became something of an institution 'round the place.

Testosterone has been the downfall of many a good male and independent though Barny may have been, he wasn't proofed against cute fillies. It was a packhorse mare Dick and I had out there, that proved his undoing.

We were riding back to the hut after work one afternoon, when we saw Barny in the high fenced holding paddock built onto the cattle yards near our camp. He was paying court through the rails to his lady love who was shut in the stockyards. As soon as the wily bugger spotted us, he wheeled 'round and went out through the open gate like his tail was on fire.

That afternoon, we got a coil of fencing wire that was in the lean to behind the hut, tied it to the bottom of the gate and ran it out to a little ridge that ended about three hundred metres from the yards. We threw dirt over the wire where it crossed the gateway and next day we came home up the back of the little ridge and peeped over to see if Barny had come-a-calling.

He was in there, so I held our horses and kept them quiet while Dick sneaked up to the end of the wire and heaved the gate shut. It was as easy as that. We'd yarded the station rogue.

Dick looked at me and I looked at Dick. *'Well we've got him. What the hell are we going to do with him?'*

Horses are usually broken in before they are over four years old. After that, they get tough, set in their ways, and can be fairly hard to handle. Just the same older horses can be trained, and we were both young and silly with plenty of time on our hands.

We ran Barny up the race and spent a bit of time rubbing him all over. He was pretty wild, but after a bit, he settled down and let us handle him. We put a halter and headrope on him and let him out into one of the yards where we pulled him 'round to the left and right and in a couple of days, we had him leading.

We bagged him down with a saddle blanket and flapped oilskins and things 'round him 'till he must have decided to indulge our childish games, and put up with us.

Over the next week or so, while we waited for the snow, Dick and I played 'round with Barny every afternoon. We saddled him, put a bit in his mouth, drove him 'round a lot using a couple of ropes for driving reins, and finally we got him to the stage where we couldn't put it off any longer. Someone was going to have to get on his back.

We tossed a coin for the job and I lost. Next day, Dick held his head with a lead rope on his halter under the bridle and I gingerly eased myself into the saddle. I got my feet in the stirrups, gathered up the reins and Dick tried to lead Barny quietly away.

Barny had been prepared to put up with our nonsense up to now, but this latest indignity was more than his independent spirit could stand.

He ripped the lead rope out of Dick's hands and 'round the yard he went bucking like a horse possessed. I reckon I did alright to last as long as I did, but he pounded me loose, and Christ that frozen ground was hard.

We all know the rule about getting back on a horse that's thrown you, so we caught Barny and I had another go. Same result. After I'd gone off as many times as I could stand, Dick decided maybe I'd worn him down a bit and he'd give him a try.

Barny didn't seem to be particularly wear-downable, because half an hour later, Dick picked himself off the ground for the sixth time and we gave Barny best for now and went up to the hut to re-think our horse breaking technique.

Next day, we put the packsaddle on him with the pack boxes filled with sand, tied everything down with straps and surcingles and turned our buckjumper loose in the yard. Old Barny bucked 'till he was too buggered to buck any more, but he couldn't shift those packs.

We retired to the hut in high good humour and spent the evening congratulating ourselves on our superior horse handling method.

We put the packs on again next day and Barny walked away with them. No problem. We put a riding saddle on and I got on. Bang! Flat on my back again with a few new bruises on top of the old ones.

We had our teeth into the project by this time and were completely committed to the idea of seeing the look on our boss, Ray Parker's face when we rode the station rogue nobody had been able to yard, back to the homestead.

There was a little mountain lake, or tarn as they call them, about half a mile from the hut with a good skin of ice over it. Next afternoon we led Barny over there with a good long rope on his halter. After a bit of coaxing, we got him out on the ice, and I held the rope while Dick got on him bareback.

Poor old Barny never had a chance. Every time he tried to buck, he slipped all over the place and fell over. Dick would slip off 'till we got him up and fly on him again. Dick rode him on the ice and I rode him on the ice. He got to the stage where he just sat on the ice and refused to move at all, so we sledged him over to the shore. I hopped on him, he got up and Dick led him back to the yards. He walked along like a dream. We'd done it!

We rode Barny 'round a bit in the following days and most of the time, he went alright, but now and again, he'd take it into his head to have a bit of a go. However, we'd definitely taken the edge off him and we both managed to stick on his back when he bucked from then on.

About a week after that, the snow arrived and we packed up and rode back into the station. We put the packs on Barny and about a mile from the homestead, we changed them over to the mare who'd had a real easy trip this far. We tossed to see who rode him in, and I lost again, only this time, it was a win. The look on the faces of Ray Parker and the rest of the family and workers when I rode Barny up to the house gate, was worth a year's wages.

When the weather warmed up after winter, Ray got the vet out and had Barny gelded. Although he was unreliable to ride and would buck whenever the mood took him, he was a real good packhorse.

Dick and I went meat hunting next summer and Ray lent us Barny to pack the deer out. He carried some bloody big loads for us. I've still got an old photo of Barney with five deer on him, which is a pretty fair load for any horse.

I've broken in a lot of horses since then and made a better job of them than Dick and I did with Barny, but he and I will always remember that winter in the New Zealand back country when two eighteen year old boys broke in a twelve year old feral stallion.

Bill's Feral Sheep

I was yarning at the saleyards with John the other day.
They were calling bids on three rams in a pen.
They were just a waste of wethers I felt compelled to say.
I've seen rougher, but I can't remember when.

John leaned against a rail with a strange look in his eye
And said '*I'm here to make sure those things sell.*
I've squared the meatworks buyer and mate, I'll tell you why
I want them rams to go to Ovine Hell.'

'*I shore those feral mongrels. It took ten years off me life*
and nearly busted up a family.
Me kids and dog all hate me. Things are dicey with the wife.
Them sheep caused it but the family's blaming me.'

They were knocked down to the butcher. John's face broke out in smiles
where before his features seemed so drawn and pale.
'*Let's go and have a cuppa mate and yarn a little while*
and I'll tell you the sad and sorry tale.'

'*I used to like that bloke called Bill who rang a week ago.*
He said he had three sheep for me to shear.
I'd never shorn for Hobby Farmers so how was I to know
the prospect should have turned me weak with fear.'

'*I turned up to shear them thinking they'd be in the yard*
though Bill had told me that he'd be at work.
After half an hour of chasing I was sweating fairly hard
convinced that good old Bill was just a jerk.'

'*You know I'm not a quitter and I said I'd do the job*
so home I went to get me dog and son
then back we went to Bill's place to muster up the 'mob'.
As things turned out I should 'a brought a gun.'

'*I put the dog around them and that mighty flock of three*
crashed the boundary fence just like it wasn't there
then they vanished in a forest that was near too thick to see.
A forest that was mostly prickly pear.'

'The mob of three was pretty soon all in three different mobs.
The dog went howling through the cactus patch.
Pulling prickles from his paws became a full time job,
and we still had three feral rams to catch.'

'We thought we'd let them settle so we sat under a tree
to wait until they ventured out again.
In about an hour like scrub bulls, they slipped out furtively.
Sneaking out to feed upon the plain.'

'I waited where I was while young Chris sneaked around the back
so we could cut their best line of retreat,
then man and son and dog erupted, charging in a pack
and pounced upon Bill's bloody feral sheep.'

'One ram and Chris dissolved like smoke back into the pear.
I was wrestling mine, but still I saw them go.
That sheep was packing Chris along as if he wasn't there
like a mutton buster at the Rodeo.'

'I fought on despite the prickles that were piercing me in scores.
Ram and dog went in the dam at breakneck run.
I watched them throw a bow wave up like ten artesian bores
with more holes in me than a punk rocker's tongue.'

'I looped me belt around his horns and tied him to a tree
then followed Chris while holding up me jeans.
With me so full of prickles, Lord knows how he would be.
Still, he's a tough one for a lad just in his teens.'

'Chris came stumbling from the pear patch saying 'Dad. Go take a hike!
I'll send dear brother Jason to help you.
I've tied him up in there and I'm off home to get de-spiked
and with these sheep, you know what you can do.'

'We had two mongrels captured and an island in the dam
made a prison for the one the dog had bailed.
Jason came 'round on the agbike grinning like an open clam
to find me pulling cactus from me tail.'

'We sent the dog to move the ram marooned out in the dam.
He swam to shore. I said a prayer of thanks
and I landed him a good kick in his feral flamin' can
then collapsed in sheer exhaustion on the bank.'

'We got them home and shore them, and old mate, I'd rather shear
ten thousand droughted wethers in the west.
Now the thought of Hobby Farmers fills me with a mortal fear
and their sheep should be declared as noxious pests.'

Our Flag

There's a hue and cry and furor in every local rag
Throughout this wide brown land of ours, about our country's flag!
Sure, let's be a Republic within Australia's shore,
But just what have we been doing for thirty years or more?

England joined the Common Market 'round nineteen sixty eight.
As far as Aussie is concerned, that's when they shut the gate!
Those lousy pommies quit us, we were independent then!
Don't think about a new flag — just think about the men.

The men who fought and died beneath that grand old Aussie rag.
The Union Jack means nothing! It's the Cross that makes the flag.
The Southern Cross that stands proud in our sky here every night.
How many Aussies died for her, to give us all the right

To adopt it as Australian — make that flag our own?
When Britain sent her convicts here, Republic's seeds were sown.
The very fact they sent them here against the will of all
Laid the slab for Aussie martyrs like Ned Kelly and Ben Hall.

Just think what it has come to mean — the navy blue and white —
From the red of Flanders poppies to a black Vietnam night.
In Pacific and North Africa it flew at our side —
Shell torn, at times blood splattered, as Aussies fought and died.

So think all you modern thinkers. Are your hearts made of stone?
Generations of Australians have made this flag their own.
Why fix something that's not broken? Why argue with the toss?
Australians have lived and died beneath the Southern Cross.

We look forward to the time when every person in this land
Behind Australia and her flag will all united, stand.
From statesmen of two thousand, to Van Dieman's oldest lag,
Let's all unite in one proud voice, and raise *Australia's flag!*

Songs of Our Australia

Rhythms of Australia throbbing out across the years.
Heartbeat of our Nation sounding easy on the ears.
Strains of Aussie music from a wailing sad guitar.
Children of the southland chase our shining Aussie star.
Songs of bold bushrangers, songs of convicts hewing stone.
Tempos of the dreamtime in their ancient pulsing tone.
Anzacs fought like tigers for our triumphs and our sins.
Music of this Nation. It is written in the wind.

CHORUS

You're an Aussie. Hear the music. Heart and soul of this great land.
You're an Aussie hear the music written by an Aussie's hand.
Let the songs of our Australia ring beneath the southern sky.
Let the songs of our Australia help Australian souls to fly.

Aussie entertainers in those early days were born
crooners of the cattle camps, sheds where sheep were shorn.
In the little towns and hamlets of the pioneer age
somebody would hoist himself onto a makeshift stage.
That's how we got the singers, the showmen and the lairs.
Not always the answer to a righteous mother's prayers.
They'd recite their poem.   Sing their newly written song
about an Aussie hero and the Law that done him wrong.

Music as Australian as the wattle in the breeze.
Forget the imitators serving masters overseas.
Tempos of our Nation spur you on to make your stand.
Let their soaring rhythms sing the glory of this land.
Stars who are our icons to the busker in the street,
Carry our tradition. Sprinkle stardust at their feet.
Love of our Australia in the beat of every song.
Clap your hands and stamp your feet. C'mon let's sing along!

Free Verse

There seems to be a tendency amongst the highbrow mob
To sneer at rhyming verse as not quite equal to the job.
And I can't fathom the objection. It's a mystery to me
When words lack rhyme and rhythm. How can it be poetry?

The origins of poetry are buried deep in time.
Didn't the old masters write with rhythm and with rhyme?
Did Tennyson and Byron find the matching couplet hard?
And we find a flowing symmetry in sonnets of the Bard.

Few attend their highbrow readings and fewer buy their books
But they still subject Bush Poets to sneers and scathing looks.
So it has me rather baffled how at any other time
The hallmark of the poet was their knack of writing rhyme.

I suppose I'm just a bumpkin but I can't applaud a style
Where a line will carry one word while the next runs half a mile.
And you stumble through it haltingly and curse its lack of flow.
But I'm obviously missing something intellectuals know.

So what can be this quality that cultured people see
That is flying o'er the thick head of a country boy like me?
Ha! I think I've found the answer! It's been there all the time.
So-called intellectuals are too dumb to make words rhyme!

The Curse of the Poet

The contest was on Saturday and steeled for the test
I paid my entry. I'd be there to mix it with the best.
This verse of mine had what it takes to make an epic poem.
For all past mediocrity this surely would atone.

Champ. Open Original. The crown I longed to wear.
Bush fires, flooded rivers notwithstanding, I'd be there
To best the leading wordsmiths, competition tough and hard,
To wear the winner's laurels and declare myself a bard.

I fairly reeked with confidence. No doubt could drag me down.
This day was fated to be mine. I'd surely wear the crown.
I got there with an hour to spare and slowly strolled about
While running through my masterpiece – the winner beyond doubt.

I would join the inner circle. Be admitted to the Bar.
For today I'd be the nemesis of poets near and far.
I strode straight out upon the stage exhibiting the signs
Of a winner as I stood there, AND FORGOT MY BLOODY LINES.

The Apprentice Dentists

If you'd met my cousin Nigel, you would have soon agreed
with me and all the kids that I ran with.
He was just the sort of sissy no gang of bush kids need.
all golden curls and pansy little lisp.

But we got stuck with Nigel at Christmas every year
when his bludging parents showed up at the farm.
His mummy would expect us to amuse the little dear
and keep her precious darling boy from harm.

He couldn't ride or swim or fish. He wasn't game to try.
Was dead-set useless setting rabbit traps.
If he didn't have a blister, he had something in his eye,
but ditch him, you'd cop my Mum with her strap.

One year in December when they turned up right on cue
Nigel had a loose tooth in his jaw.
In matters dental us kids knew exactly what to do.
We'd seen Dad knock horse's wolf teeth out before.

No one consulted Nigel. He could simply cop his fate.
We sat him on an upturned kero tin
for the boys and I determined it was time to operate.
We opened up his gob and peered within.

Clarry Murphy grabbed a mallet and a flat screwdriver too
while Nigel started squeaking with alarm.
When Clarry lined the molar up the little wimp shot through,
but we tackled him before he fled the barn.

We settled him with stories of cashed up tooth fairies
and terrifying tales of gangrene.
We were saviours who just wanted Nigel's discomfort to ease.
We'd use fishing line and jerk the thing out clean.

We tied a noose around the tooth and sat him near the door.
Tied the handle to the loose end of the gut.
But we'd never seen old Nigel move so bloody quick before
He hit that door before Mick slammed it shut.

So I untied the line and towed me cousin 'round the back.
He led along so tame it made us laugh.
Right up to a ladder leant against a big hay stack
just like a halter broken poddy calf.

Then I went up the ladder Nigel following just fine,
while Clarry looked around to find a stone.
He was right there at me heels never tightening the line
but up on top the sook began to moan.

'I want my tooth to thay in and my poor headth weally thore'
he cried while Clarry came up with a rock.
He wouldn't have a bruised scone if he hadn't hit the door.
So we just told him where to put the sock.

We led him by the string up to the far end of the stack,
tied the loose end to the stone that Clarry found.
When we chucked the rock off it should have jerked the slack
but Nigel jumped and beat it to the ground.

Scream! You've never heard the like. It echoed 'round the farm.
Mum and Dad showed up and we were dead.
The sooky little mongrel only had a broken arm
and the flamin' tooth was still inside his head.

They took Nigel to the doctor.   Mick and Clarry got sent home
and my bum got a taste of my Dad's boot.
I spent the rest of Nigel's visit burr chipping on me own
plotting vengeance on that whinging little coot.

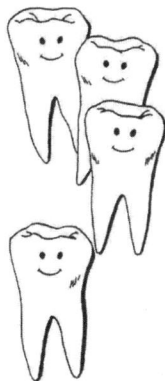

Woody's Mongrel Breed

If I said he was a nice dog, I'd be only telling lies
because Woody was a mongrel in near anybody's eyes.
Still I wished I'd got a pup by him. He had a certain charm,
like the smile on a crocodile before it eats your arm.

So I went down in the coast hills where I thought I'd have a show.
Woody done a lot of shaggin' down there thirteen years ago.
And outside a hippy shanty was a sign 'Blue Pups For Sale',
so I asked them for a look at both the mother and the male.

The mother was a blue bitch with a patch or two of red.
They couldn't show the father 'cause he came and loved and fled
but they said he was a bluey. I had all the proof I need.
I'd stumbled on a strain of Woody's good old mongrel breed.

I looked that litter over, hanging back a little way
and tried to pick a good 'un as I watched the pups at play.
When I walked up towards them, one stood up and growled.
I thought '*You're the one for me Mate. You'll do old Woody proud.*'

So I parted with a hundred. He was cheap at twice the price
And by the look of them poor hippy kids, some tucker'd be nice.
So with everyone a winner, I got back in the ute
with this fairly agro ball of fluff – a bloody little beaut.

Then back towards the mountains me and Woody Junior went
Till I saw a chance that seemed to me it must be heaven sent.
A sign 'For Sale Rottweiler Pups', in a flash Gold Coast suburb
'Inoculated, Champion Lines' and all that breeder's blurb.

It's funny how some dog breeders look more like dogs than dogs
and this one would look quite at home hunting feral hogs.
She released a fair sized litter to let them run around
and I opened up the ute door and put Woody on the ground.

Now when those little ears pricked up, I knew I had the goods.
A low growl rumbled in his throat just like his Grandad would.
He lifted up a front foot and his whole stance seemed to say
'*I'll have yez all on, in a bunch or any other way.*'

With much abuse and posturing, the fight got set to start
then the little Aussie battler took those big Germans apart.
A raging dose of blue salts in a blur of snarl and snap,
his little milk teeth working like a berserk rabbit trap.

His fluffy back hair standing up like soldiers in a row,
National pride surged through me as the Aussie had a go.
The black and tans were screaming, rolling over on their backs
as pints of puppy piddle laid the dust upon the track.

And each Rottweiler puppy was so glad about the fact
that their little baby tails were yet to face cruel fashion's axe.
The blueing blue struck terror in those young Germanic hearts
and baby tails clamped down on immature private parts.

The rout was short and brutal and it looked like time to scoot.
I grabbed Bruce Lee incarnate and we bolted for the ute.
As the breeder lumbered towards me yelling I was bloody scum,
She looked more like a Rottie than those scattered puppies' mum.

I leaped behind the wheel and as we roared out of that place
I saw Woody's sleazy smirk across his little Grandson's face,
and I reached across to pat him, but I should 'a been awake.
He latched on to me finger like a flamin' Tiger Snake.

We went back to the ranges and my joy was unrestrained.
I knew I had a canine fit to grace old Woody's chain.
A natural born blue ratbag with a style all his own.
The good old days were back again when Woody's breed came home.

About the Author

Jack Drake is a product of the bush, who has lived the life he writes about. He has straightened up at the end of eight hours on a shearing board and twisted his handpiece off ready for a well earned beer.

He knows the satisfaction of riding a horse for a day's mustering, he has bred and broken-in, with a saddle he has made himself. Like most bush boys, he can handle shoeing tools, fencing gear, carpentry and welding equipment and turn his hand to any of the hundred and one tasks necessary for survival in the bush.

Born in rural New Zealand in 1950, he is now a naturalised Aussie and proud of it. He has loved words and verse ever since his father gave him a copy of Banjo Paterson's verses when he was 10 years old.

Jack recites his own works plus other bush favourites, with fire and gusto to the delight of his audiences both old and young. His life long experience with horses, sheep, cattle and all bush things, adds a ring of authenticity to his renditions.

Jack is a regular performer at festivals and events around Queensland and New South Wales and has recited his works at the Gympie Muster Poets Breakfasts for the last four years and performed at Tamworth Country Music Week for the last five years.

His wins in Bush Poetry Competitions include:

- The Asthma Foundation of NSW's 'Bush Poet of the Year 2001' in Sydney on 30.4.2001.

- The Tenterfield Oracles of the Bush written section in 1999 and performance section in 2000 and 2001.

- The original performance section of the National Bush Poetry Championship at the Brisbane Royal National Show 11.8.2001

- Placings in many other regional contests.

- His C.D. "The Cattle Dog's Revenge" was a finalist in the 2002 Australian Bush Laureate Awards at Tamworth.

- His C.D. "Dinkum Poetry" was a finalist in the 2003 Australian Bush Laureate Awards at Tamworth

His CDs have sold as far afield as Britain, Canada, New Zealand and the United States as well as all over Australia, receiving air play on Alan Jones and John Laws radio programs as well as ABC National and a host of regional stations. A piece of Jack's poetry also adorns the wall of *Café Oz* in Paris, France.